PSYCHOACTIVE CACTI

THE PSYCHEDELIC EFFECTS OF MESCALINE IN PEYOTE, SAN PEDRO, & THE PERUVIAN TORCH

ALEX GIBBONS

UPDATES

For a chance to go into the draw to win a FREE book every month like our 'Stoner Themed Coloring Book' (below), and other updates on our latest books, subscribe below!

https://psychedeliccuriosity.activehosted.com/f/1

For daily posts on all things Psychedelic, follow us on Instagram @Psychedelic.curiosity

DISCLAIMER

We do not condone the use of peyote or any other mescaline cacti. Growing, buying and selling mescaline cacti might be considered as criminal activities in your state or country, so if you engage in any of these activities, you would probably be doing so at the risk of imprisonment. We strongly discourage you from engaging in drug possession, drug distribution, and drug dealing. This book is meant for informational and entertainment purposes only, and we bear no responsibility for any decisions that you make as an individual with regard to mescaline and other controlled substances.

CONTENTS

In consciousness dwells the wondrous, with it man attains the realm beyond the material, and the Peyote tells us, where to find it.

— ANTONIN ARTAUD

INTRODUCTION

In the chapters that follow, you will learn everything you need to about mescaline and the various cacti from which it is sourced.

We will discuss the history of mescaline use. We will then look at the most common mescaline cacti, one by one, and help you understand everything you need to know about where they can be found, how to identify them, and what to expect from these plants.

We will then get a little bit technical. We will discuss techniques used to prepare mescaline, and that will involve a little knowledge of chemistry. We will also look at the working mechanism of mescaline in the brain and the body. We've simplified the technical explanations as much as possible, so even if you are not that into science, you will have an easy time understanding this section.

After that, we will discuss the spiritual and psychological implications of mescaline use, along with other benefits of using mescaline. We will top that off with a discussion of the potential negative effects of mescaline, and what you can do to prevent a bad mescaline trip.

Finally, we will look at practical mescaline use in the real world through two educational mescaline trip reports.

WHAT IS MESCALINE?

Mescaline is a psychoactive substance that is naturally found in some species of desert cacti that are native to North, Central, and South America. There are many different types of cacti that contain mescaline, but the most common ones are the peyote cacti, the Peruvian Torch cacti, the San Pedro cacti, and the Bolivian Torch cacti. Mescaline is also naturally found in certain types of wild beans, but the concentrations are too low to create any psychoactive effects.

Mescaline has many functions in fields such as botany, organic chemistry, and medicine, but for the purposes of this book, we will look at mescaline as a psychedelic drug. We aim to provide educational and actionable information for those looking to understand how they can take advantage of its psychoactive properties. However, the fact is that your understanding of mescaline wouldn't be complete if we don't at least take a look at the basic science behind it.

Mescaline belongs to a group of chemicals known as Phenethylamine alkaloids, and its chemical name is "three, four, five-trimethoxyphenethylamine." Most known phenethylamine alkaloids have profound effects on the human brain when ingested. Some stimulate the central nervous system, some are appetite suppressants, and some are antidepressants, while others, like mescaline, cause hallucinogenic effects.

Mescaline bearing cacti usually contain more than one type of phenethylamine alkaloid. Cacti such as peyote, San Pedro, and Peruvian Torch primarily contain mescaline, but they also have significant concentrations of other phenethylamines. In the case of Bolivian Torch cacti, the collective concentration of secondary phenethylamine alkaloids is so high that some argue that a Bolivian Torch trip can't be considered to be a genuine mescaline trip.

For more than a hundred years, scientists have been able to synthesize mescaline in the lab using highly controlled chemical processes. Synthetic mescaline can be found in some parts of the world as a street drug. However, most mescaline consumers still prefer natural mescaline that's extracted directly from the various types of cacti that we have listed above.

Like many other natural psychoactive plants, mescaline bearing cacti have been cultivated, processed, and consumed as mind-altering substances for generations. Native Americans have used peyote for hundreds if not thousands of years in religious rituals. Several other mescaline cacti continue to be used by tribes native to the Americas both for ritualistic and recreational purposes.

Mescaline had been used by westerners for several generations now. Like with many other mind-altering substances, the use of mescaline among European-Americans can be traced back to the hippie movement of the fifties, sixties, and seventies. This counterculture movement sought to rethink the rigid social norms of their times, and as part of that, they experimented with many mind-altering substances, including mescaline cacti.

Since then, the use of mescaline has spread across America and the west at a slow but steady rate. Today, mescaline is a fairly popular psychedelic substance. According to data collected by the American National Institute of Health (NIH), as of 2015, more than eight million Americans had taken mescaline for recreational purposes at some point in their lives. The data also shows a steady rise in the number of mescaline users in recent years.

When ingested in high enough concentrations, mescaline induces a psychedelic state. This psychedelic state is similar in some ways to those induced by psilocybin or LSD, but it has some unique characteristics. Many people who have tripped on high concentrations of mescaline recall experiencing an altered sense of self, a warped sense of time, a change in their thinking processes, and closed and open-eyed visuals.

Although there are common threads that underlie most recorded mescaline trips, no two trips are exactly the same. As you will learn in the course of this book, mescaline trips are highly subjective. If you trip on mescaline, your experience will be affected by your emotional state, physical location, dosage, among many other factors. Because of this, it's hard to conceive of a "template" mescaline trip, but that's the beauty of the whole thing. When you take mescaline, you go on a journey that you can't completely predict or control.

Being a psychoactive compound, the production, distribution, and use of mescaline is a controlled substance in most countries. In America, the recreational use of mescaline is prohibited, but Native Americans are allowed to use peyote and other cacti for religious rituals. Still, in some states, you can buy a mescaline cactus and put it in your home as an ornamental plant, or you can just wander off into the desert and forage for peyote. In most of Europe, mescaline is considered an illegal drug, but even then, enforcement isn't as strict as it is with other controlled substances.

So, the simple answer to the question "What is mescaline?" is: it is a natural, time tested, and relatively safe psychedelic that millions use for both spiritual and recreational purposes.

2

THE HISTORY OF MESCALINE

Mescaline is probably the oldest psychedelic known to man. Anthropologists have differing opinions on this matter with some arguing that the use of psilocybin (the psychoactive compound in magic mushrooms) might predate the use of peyote and other mescaline cacti. Still, it's undeniable that mescaline has been used by humans for thousands of years.

We don't know much about the exact origins of mescaline use because it predates written history. However, there is strong archaeological evidence that indicates that peyote cactus has existed for more than 10,000 years in areas inhabited by humans, mostly around modern-day Mexico and Texas. Given that humans foraged for food back then, archeologists speculate that some cave men might have eaten some peyote (supposedly for its nutrients), after which they experienced hallucinations which they interpreted through a religious or spiritual lens.

That theory has been backed up by recent findings in a

cave in Rio Grande, Texas. Archeologists discovered fossilized peyote cacti inside the cave. Carbon dating tests indicate that the cacti fossils date back to 3700 B.C. (over 5700 years ago). It's clear that the cave dwellers harvested the peyote and stored them inside the cave for later use. This is the earliest conclusive piece of evidence that links ancient American tribes to mescaline use.

There are many other pieces of evidence (mostly from a few hundred years B.C.) including stone carvings, and other forms of artwork that clearly depict the use (or the edification) of peyote by tribesmen. According to ethnobotanists and anthropologists, and archeologists, there is evidence that proves that Native Americans have always known about the psychedelic properties of peyote. Why else would they depict peyotes as these grandiose centerpieces in their works of art?

The Huichol tribe, in particular, believed that all foods were bestowed to them by God, and that foods or plants with special properties were indeed special gifts from God. Their oral narratives show that to them peyote was an extra-special divine gift, and they believed that it had magic power. Even today, members of the Huichol tribe still go on annual pilgrimages to Wirikuta (a place in Mexico), where peyote is grown on a large scale.

The written history of mescaline starts with the arrival of Spanish explorers in Mexico. In 1519, renowned explorer Hernan Cortes conquered the Aztecs, and as the Spanish made inroads into Mexico, they became aware of the widespread use of peyote for both religious and medical purposes. The Spaniards saw peyote as a threat. They noticed that locals who consumed the plant never showed any signs of fear or hunger. They were genuinely concerned that peyote might give the Aztecs the strength and courage to organize an uprising and overthrow their rule.

Even though the Spaniards had a better understanding of modern science than their Aztec counterparts, this was the sixteenth century, and almost everyone believed in magic. The Spaniards (most of whom were Catholics) were convinced that peyote had dark evil powers. Over the next century or so, the Spaniards did their best to stop the consumption of peyote in Mexico and their other central American territories, claiming that it was "witchcraft" and "the devil's work." By 1620, the use of peyote was outlawed, and any violation of that law was punishable by death.

Old traditions die hard. Despite all the efforts by the Spaniards, some native tribes kept using peyote in secret. They held ritualistic ceremonies in secluded places in the dead of night, and the Spanish were none-the-wiser. They passed their knowledge on how to prepare, consume, and experience peyote from generation to generation, and that way, this cherished native tradition survived in the underground for hundreds of years.

It's unclear when peyote first made its way to Europe, but there's strong evidence that shows explorers in the eighteenth and nineteenth centuries collected plants and cacti from all over the Americas, brought them back, and planted them in exotic botanical gardens across Europe. A German scientist and pharmacologist named Louis Lewin was the first person in Europe to extensively study and write about peyote. In 1887, he received a shipment of peyote buttons from a Texas-based doctor who wanted him to study the plant to discover if it had any medicinal value, and to further understand its psychoactive properties.

In 1896, another German doctor named Arthur Heffter, a colleague of Dr. Lewin's, was the first to isolate mescaline and identify it as the main psychoactive ingredient in peyote. Dr. Heffter and his team coined the word "mescaline" in honor of the Mescalero Apache Native American tribe because the peyote buttons used in the lab study were originally sourced from their tribal land.

In the early twentieth century, Native American tribes started to feel emboldened to practice their religious rituals unapologetically. In response to attempts by the federal government to ban the use of peyote (as part of a broader effort that led to the prohibition), Native Americans decided to use their religious freedom rights to protect their traditional practices. The Native American Church was incorporated in 1918, and from the very beginning, it was a major proponent of open peyote use. The church made it very clear that peyote was like a sacrament in their denomination, and any attempts by the American government to outlaw it, was tantamount to the violation of their religious freedoms. In the Native American Church doctrine, slices of peyote are considered the body of Christ, and the psychedelic effects of the cactus are seen as revelations or insights that can help their faithful to have a deeper communion with God. The native church had faced many challenges over the decades, but a century later, it still stands strong.

In 1919, a German chemist named Dr. Ernst Spath figured out how to make synthetic mescaline. He used raw chemicals in his lab to create pure mescaline in powder form. Since then, other chemists have figured out several other methods of synthesizing mescaline.

Starting in the 1940s, there was a growing belief around the world (especially in military and intelligence circles) that mescaline and other psychedelics could be used as truth serums. In 1945, a Nazi physician gave mescaline to prisoners at concentration camps before interrogating them to see if it made them more inclined to tell the truth. There are also reports from around the same time period which indicate that the US Office of Strategic Services (the predecessor to the CIA) also tested mescaline as a truth serum, but they stopped the experiments because it induced nausea in the subjects (which actually made them less likely to be forthcoming with any secrets that they had).

In the early 1950s, a Canadian doctor named Humphrey Osmond ran various studies where he tried to understand the similarities between adrenaline and mescaline. Dr. Osmond is the one who actually invented the term psychedelic. His study of the effects of mescaline and LSD on the brain led him to come up with new and innovative ways to treat psychiatric conditions. Inspired by Dr. Osmond's work, some intellectuals of his period became more open to the idea of using psychedelics for creative pursuits. One such person was renowned author Aldous Huxley.

In 1953, novelist Aldous Huxley started experimenting with mescaline under the careful supervision of Dr. Osmond. In one instance, he took a 400 mg dose of mescaline and went on a fascinating trip. He later published a book called "The Doors of Perception" where he described his experiences during the trip in as much detail as possible. Huxley's book is probably the most famous mescaline trip of all time. In a later edition of the same book, he explained how mescaline (and other psychedelics) can be used to gain personal insights and to discover spiritual revelations. With the success of Huxley's book, the discussion on mescaline use entered the social consciousness in America and across the west.

In the 1960s, during the hippie movement, mescaline use increased among non-native Americans, most of whom were young, open-minded people who were willing to experiment with different kinds of psychedelics. However, mescaline wasn't as popular as LSD and other synthetic psychedelics because it was relatively harder for dealers to acquire and distribute it in commercially viable volumes. This had something to do with the nature of the mescaline cacti. They tend to grow slowly, and in many cases, it takes several years for them to mature, so they don't readily lend themselves to being peddled on the streets. Still, the hippie movement laid the groundwork for the popularity of mescaline and other psychedelics in the modern era.

Another significant historical contribution of mescaline in

the 1960s was that it led to the discovery of several other psychedelics. For example, a chemist named Alexander Shulgin tripped on mescaline in 1960, and he liked it so much that he decided to dedicate his career to discovering other phenethylamines and alkaloids that may have similar effects to mescaline. A few years later, he created MDMA. Shulgin was the first to make dozens of variants of MDMA, which became popular in the dance clubs of the 1970s. To Shulgin, MDMA and its variants are just "tamed" versions of mescaline – meaning that they last a shorter time and have a milder effect than mescaline.

When the United States passed the Controlled Substance Act in 1970, it re-categorized mescaline as a Schedule I controlled substance. Substances in this category are considered to have no medicinal value, to be very unsafe, and to be potentially addictive. However, an exemption was written into that same act, and it was later affirmed in the American Indian Religious Freedoms act of 1978. Members of the Native American Church and other organizations successfully lobbied congress to allow their members to use peyote for religious purposes.

One year after America banned the use of mescaline, the United Nations held the Convention on Psychotropic Substances in which mescaline and other psychedelics were prohibited internationally.

In America, some states have tried to take away the rights of Native Americans to use peyote for spiritual purposes in recent decades. For example, the state of Oregon reintroduced restrictions after it successfully petitioned the Supreme Court to suspend some sections of the Religious

Freedoms Restoration Act in the 1990s. Since then, states have been able to set their own rules on the use of peyote by Native Americans and other people claiming to share the beliefs of Native Americans.

Other mescaline cacti (such as the Peruvian Torch and the San Pedro cactus) don't enjoy the same religious rights protections as peyote. They are either banned or restricted in most American states, but despite that, they are easily available as ornamental plants in botanical shops. It seems strange that plants which are considered illegal should be sold for ornamental purposes. This disparity came about partly because when the Controlled Substances Act was originally written, lawmakers didn't know much about the other genres and species of mescaline cacti. They just applied a blanket ban on mescaline, so anyone claiming that he or she is acquiring a mescaline cactus as a decorative plant can take advantage of a massive loophole.

In recent years, mescaline has experienced a resurgence in popularity; it's now more popular among non-native Americans than it has ever been at any point in history. That's because younger generations are more open minded than their predecessors, and they are more willing to try out mind altering substances at least once in their lives.

Today, depending on where you live, you might be able to get mescaline (in the form of dried or powdered cactus) from your friendly neighborhood dealer, or you might be able to go foraging for it out in the desert. Mescaline is mostly consumed in its natural form; synthetic mescaline has all but disappeared from the streets, but it's still manu-factured and used for scientific research.

As you can see, mescaline has a rich history that dates back several millennia, and it's a core part of a life affirming tradition. So when you trip on mescaline, you should know that you are not just having a good time, you are partaking in grand old traditions; you are a part of something bigger than you.

PEYOTE CACTI

Peyote is a small cacti that is native to the Americas. Its scientific name is *Lophophora williamsii*. Most of the plant's body grows underground, and only a small section known as the "button" actually surfaces above the soil. The peyote button is very distinctive. It has a globular shape, and it is deep green in color. On an average peyote cactus, the button grows to the size of a baseball. The button is all flesh, and it has no spine, so it can be wholly eaten.

Peyote is by far the most well-known, and the most potent of all mescaline cacti. As we've mentioned previously, it has been used by Native American tribes for millennia for its psychoactive properties and for much more. It is native to the desert areas of the North American continent, mostly Mexico and the American South West. Peyote is a Spanish word, but it's derived from the Aztec word "pey-otl" which means "shining" or "glistening." The word also means "divine messenger" in specific contexts.

The peyote button is consumed in a number of different

ways. Firstly it can be eaten raw. Secondly, it can be brewed into a sort of tea. Thirdly, it can be dried, crushed into a powder, and packaged into capsules. Fourthly, the dried peyote can be crumbled and rolled into cigarettes which can be smoked. A person's choice of mode of consumption will depend on their own personal preferences, and the nature of the trip that they want to experience.

Peyote is a strange type of cactus. Without spines or thorns, it seems like a delicate plant that typically wouldn't survive in the desert. However, botanists have theorized that peyote developed mescaline as a survival mechanism. You see, mescaline causes a severe negative reaction in most animals, so they avoid eating wild peyote, leaving the plant to thrive in an otherwise harsh environment. Since most of the plant is underground, it can store large reserves of water within its roots, without having to lose it all because of the scorching desert sun. This way, the peyote buttons seem like desert flowers that bud right out of the ground looking green and healthy in contrast with the brown withering desert vegetation all around.

Peyote mostly grows among desert scrub in clusters, although it's not uncommon to find an isolated button. If you stumble on peyote out in nature, most of the time, it will look like a group of flattened spheroids of different sizes, clustered right on the ground. Most will be green, but some will be golden yellowish in color. The top of the buttons appear sunken throughout most of the year. In the seasons between March and May, the top of each peyote button blossoms into a pinkish, yellowish, or whitish flower. For those who go foraging for peyote out in the desert, this is the best season for it because they are much easier to spot.

Peyote flowers grow into small pink colored fruits, which are also edible and contain mescaline. The fruits are elongated and they are shaped like clubs. They start out with a rosy color, but as they mature, they turn brownish or eggshell white. When busted open, the inside of the mature peyote fruit contains black seeds. If the peyote is left undisturbed, the fruit will eventually fall off, and the seeds will germinate under hot and humid conditions, thus propagating the peyote cactus.

If you come across a fruit bearing peyote plant in the desert, the ethical thing to do would be to save the seeds and not waste them. You should either bury the seeds in the ground and give them a chance to grow, or you can take them with you and try to grow them in a pot at home under the right conditions (remember to ensure that you aren't caught breaking any laws in your state).

Peyote takes a very long time to grow out in nature. Even in cultivated gardens or farms, peyote can take more than three years to grow from mere seedlings to mature flowering cacti. This poses a serious challenge to anyone who wants to mass produce the cacti. In fact, due to a combination of its slow growth and an increasing demand from those looking to trip on mescaline, peyote has landed on the list of endangered plant species. Some botanists have devised grafting techniques that can be used to increase the growth rate and yield of peyote. Now, it's possible to graft peyote onto the root stock of San Pedro cacti.

In areas such as south Texas, wild peyote has been over-harvested, and the plant's population has been seriously decimated. That's because most people looking for the plant in the wilderness don't take the time to learn the proper harvesting technique, and they end up killing the peyote.

When harvesting peyote out in the desert (or even farmed or potted peyote), there is a proper technique involved. You want to ensure that you get the edible part of the cactus while ensuring that you don't kill the plant itself. You have to cut off the peyote button at the top of the root in one clean continuous cut. This way the root is left with a smooth surface. Overtime, a callous will form on the surface, and the cut will heal. The peyote will then grow another button, and it will keep thriving. You don't need to pull out the whole plant because the root doesn't have much mescaline (and is therefore useless to you). If you care about nature, you should take what you need from the cactus, and let it keep on living.

Pharmacologically, peyote contains more than sixty different types of alkaloids. Most of these alkaloids are psychoactive. However, they exist in the plant only in trace amounts. Mescaline is the one alkaloid that is in a high enough concentration to have actual psychoactive effects when peyote is ingested. Some of the other significant alkaloids in peyote include tyramine, hordenine, anhaloni-dine, and pellotine. It's important to take note of these alkaloids because when peyote is ingested in high amounts (like in the instance of a heroic dose), they tend to add up, so you have to ensure that you don't have any health conditions, or you aren't on any medication that may be contraindicated with these alkaloids.

Native Americans believe that peyote has medicinal properties (apart from its psychoactive properties). Native medicine men use peyote to treat all sorts of ailments, including toothaches, skin diseases, fever, and the common cold, diabetes, and chest pain. They also use peyote during delivery to help with labor pains. In some tribes, it's even believed that peyote can temporarily cure blindness. Of course, none of these claims have been proven by modern science, but if the Native Americans and the Aztecs have been using peyote for medicinal purposes for thousands of years, maybe there's something to it.

The effects you'll experience after taking peyote will mostly depend on the dosage. A typical light dose of peyote for an adult will range from 1.75 ounces to 5.35 ounces (fifty to a hundred grams) in case you eat fresh peyote, or 0.35 to 0.7 ounces (ten to twenty grams) in case you ingest dried peyote. If you take a dose lower than 1.75 ounces (fifty grams) fresh or 0.35 ounces (ten grams) dried of peyote, it's highly likely that you won't experience any significant psychoactive effects.

Moderate doses of peyote range from 3.5 to 5.3 ounces (a hundred to 150 grams) for fresh peyote or 0.7 to 1 ounce (twenty to thirty grams) for dried peyote. Strong doses of peyote range from 5.3 to 7 ounces (150 to 200 grams) for fresh peyote or one to 1.4 ounces (thirty to forty grams) of dried peyote. Any dose higher than 7 ounces (200 grams) fresh or 1.4 ounces (forty grams) dried of peyote, is considered a "heroic dose." Unless you have a lot of experience taking hallucinogens, it's not advisable to go that high. If you are on your first trip, a light or moderate dose would suffice.

It's also important to note that peyote varies in potency, depending on the area where it's sourced, the growing condition, and even the specific variety (subspecies) of the peyote. Older peyote plants also tend to have more mescaline than younger ones because they have had more time to naturally synthesize the hallucinogenic. The season during which the peyote is harvested also matters; peyote buttons harvested during winter tend to be the most potent.

Unless you are a trained botanist, it's difficult to gauge the exact concentration of the peyote that you are taking, but that is not especially important. You don't have to be all scientific about it. You don't need an exact dosage to have the trip that you are hoping for; as long as you are in the right ballpark, you will do just fine.

The effects of peyote last about ten to twelve hours on average. That includes the come up, the trip itself, and the comedown. If you are planning on tripping on peyote for recreational purposes, you might want to make sure that you clear your calendar for at least twenty four hours to avoid a situation where the trip (or the after effects) collide with your life responsibilities.

Thirty minutes after ingesting peyote, most people start to experience physiological distress, particularly in their digestive system. This is completely normal, and it's something that you should be psychologically prepared for. Just as the peyote starts to kick in, it's highly likely that you will feel nauseated and very uncomfortable. You may feel like your stomach is excessively full. You may also sweat profusely, and/or experience chills. Even people who have been on multiple peyote trips still experience these reactions during subsequent trips.

The feelings of physiological distress usually last between one and two hours. When you feel nauseated at first, you might want to try to fight the urge to vomit, until most of the mescaline has been absorbed into your system. However, many people end up vomiting despite their best efforts, so if you are taking the peyote indoors, you should make sure that you have quick and easy access to the bathroom, or at least have a designated vomit bucket right next to you.

Roughly two hours after ingesting peyote, you should be free and clear. The bad physical reactions will go away, and the psychoactive reactions will come to a clearer focus. Of course, the psychoactive experiences will be totally subjective, but they are rarely anywhere as negative at the physiological distress that you experience in the first couple of hours.

A typical peyote trip will reach its peak between two and four hours after ingestion. Depending on the dosage that you are on, you will experience profound alterations in your perceptions, you will have strong and intense emotional reactions, and you may be highly suggestible. If your dosage is on the stronger end of the spectrum, you may question the nature of your reality, or experience alternative realities altogether.

There are vastly different reports out there on people's experiences during peyote trips. There are those who feel one with nature, there are those who experience ego-death, and there are yet others who stumble upon life changing or life affirming realizations during their trips. There is no way to predict how your peyote trip is going to turn out, but based on other peoples accounts, chances are that you will experience visual effects (such as seeing vivid colors, distortions, and geometrical patterns).

After your peyote trip peaks, it's going to decline gradually over the next eight hours or so. Serious hallucinations will only occur during the peak. After that, things will taper off, until all psychoactive effects totally disappear. After the effects are gone, it will take a few more hours before you feel completely normal again.

Peyote has been praised in scientific literature for its therapeutic effects. In fact, it is currently being studied as a possible intervention for people with alcohol and substance abuse problems. There is anecdotal evidence that shows that peyote can help treat alcohol addiction. The prevalence of alcohol addiction among Native Americans is twice the national average in America, but it is very low among those who are members of the Native American Church which uses peyote as a sacrament. While many have pointed to this as evidence that peyote reduces alcoholism, some have argued that it's the sense of community fostered by the Native American church that really reduces the incidence of alcoholism among its members.

In theory, peyote can help alcoholics to hit rock bottom in

a visual sense, without having to really do it in real life, and that is crucial to recovery. Peyote is known to induce visions, and to make people suggestible. A skilled therapist can guide an alcoholic on a peyote trip through a meditation process in which he or she can visualize his or her own eventual ruin. This will create a sense of urgency in the addict, and he or she is therefore more likely to take steps towards recovery. Peyote can also make alcoholics more self-aware, and dismantle their denial mechanisms, making them accept their reality (which is step one in the recovery process).

Numerous studies on the safety and toxicity of peyote have indicated that the plant does not have any detrimental long-term effects to the health of those who use it. One study conducted in 2005 tested dozens of native Americans who had been using peyote for decades, and none of them seemed to have any physiological or psychological problems that could be linked back to mescaline or peyote.

However, it's crucial to note that mescaline can be unsafe if it's taken in the wrong context. Just like any other mind-altering substance, peyote can affect your judgement, and it can lead you to take certain actions that could result in you getting harmed. When tripping on peyote, you might want to ensure that you are in a safe place.

If you want to go foraging for peyote out in the desert, we strongly recommend that you bring someone with you, or that you do it in a group. If you ingest peyote buttons while alone out in the wilderness you may find yourself on a trip so strong that you are unable to find your way out of the desert. You could be exposed to the elements, or attacked by wild animals. It's great to commune with nature, but at least make sure that someone knows where you are before you venture off alone in the wilderness.

Some Native Americans believe that peyote can be categorized into two; "peyote of the God," and "peyote of the Goddess." If you are taking peyote for religious purposes, this distinction might be important to you. However, if you are taking it for recreational purposes, botanists have confirmed that the distinction between the two is just superficial, and peyotes are all just the same.

There is also a cactus that belongs to the same genus as peyote. It only has trace amounts of mescaline, so it doesn't have the same psychoactive effects. It looks physically similar to peyote in many ways, and it's popularly referred to as "false peyote." If you are purchasing a potted peyote plant, you might want to watch out for scammers who might want to pawn off this fake peyote on you.

4

PERUVIAN TORCH CACTI

The Peruvian Torch cactus has two scientific names:
Trichocereus perivianus, and *Echinopsis periviana*. The former
was the original scientific name, and the latter is more up-
to-date, but both names are acceptable in scientific literature about the cactus. As its colloquial name suggests, the
cactus is native to Peru, particularly in the western slopes
of the Andes. The Peruvian Torch cactus contains several
alkaloids in minor or insignificant concentrations, but
mescaline stands out as the main alkaloid in its stem.

Just like peyote, Peruvian Torch use predates the arrival of
Europeans in the Americas. Archeological evidence indicates that natives in Peru have been using the cactus for
religious and medicinal purposes as far back as 900 BC.
Way before the establishment of the Incan Empire in
South America, monks were using Peruvian cactus (and
other types of mescaline cacti in the region) to brew
various concoctions such as "cimora", "huachuma" and
"achuma". These concoctions were often given to sick
people to treat various ailments. The monks themselves

would partake in the consumption of the beverages as a way of getting in touch with the divine.

Today, Peruvian Torch is one of the most readily available natural sources of mescaline. It grows faster than most other mescaline cacti, which makes it the species of choice for those who want to mass produce mescaline for commercial purposes. It also has a higher mescaline potency than other cacti (with the exception of peyote). It is easily found in botanical shops, and it's often cultivated by those seeking to have easy access to mescaline cacti in their own homes.

If you buy dried or fresh mescaline cacti off the street, it's highly likely to be of the Peruvian Torch variety. For dealers, Peruvian Torch is less risky because it doesn't have the same legal restrictions as peyote. It also grows to such a large mass that one stem can be subdivided into many doses (recall that peyote grown in small buttons, and you may need several buttons to get a decent dose of mescaline).

Peruvian Torch is green in color, though it has a bluish hue. The stems are columnar in shape, and the skin looks frosted. Under the right conditions, in its wild and natural habitat, the columnar stems can grow up to about ten to twenty feet (three to six meters) tall. The diameter of the columns can be anywhere between three and seven inches (eight and eighteen centimeters) for a mature Peruvian Torch cactus. The cacti always start out straight, but some of them tend to arch a bit as they grow taller and heavier. In some rare cases, Peruvian Torches can get so heavy that their stems arch all the way down and the plant lies flat on the ground.

For the untrained eye, it can be quite difficult to distinguish between the Peruvian Torch and other types of cacti out there. This particular type of cactus has between four and eight ribs. The ribs are usually in even numbers, so they give the cactus a symmetrical appearance. Each rib has spines that range from an eggshell color, all the way to a dark brown color. The spines are clustered in groups of six to eight, and those clusters are evenly spaced along the edge of the spine; they are roughly one inch apart. The spines can grow to a length of 1.6 inches (four centimeters). Older cacti tend to have longer and sturdier spines while younger cacti have shorter and softer spines.

What makes the Peruvian Torch cacti quite difficult to identify out in the wilderness, is the fact that it exists in at least twelve different varieties. These varieties have subtle differences that can be confusing to a forager. The good news is that all the varieties have considerable concentrations of mescaline, so whichever one you come across, you can be assured that it's going to be good enough for your trip.

The main problem with Peruvian Torch cactus is that the concentration of mescaline varies greatly from one plant to the next. There are lots of unpredictable genetic and physical differences that lead to higher or lower doses of mescaline in any Peruvian Torch cactus. The concentration of mescaline may be affected by the genetic traits of the individual plant, and environmental conditions where the cactus grows (e.g. availability of water, the temperature, exposure to direct sunlight, the nature of the soil, etc.).

The variations in mescaline concentration are so great, that it's hard to estimate the amount of fresh Peruvian Torch that you would have to take to experience a certain kind of trip. In fact, some Peruvian Torch cacti (both from Peru and from Europe) have been found to contain no mescaline at all. In other similar studies, the mescaline content in European Peruvian Torch was found to only exist in trace amounts.

You can see the challenge that you are up against if you are trying to acquire a Peruvian Torch cactus for recreational use. First, it's hard to tell if you have the right species. Secondly, even if you have the right species, there is no guarantee that your plant contains enough mescaline for a decent trip. You can mitigate against these uncertainties by sourcing your Peruvian Torch cacti (whether live, fresh or dried) from a reliable dealer or distributor. Many users start out by acquiring small samples of Peruvian Torch, to begin with, and then increasing their cash investment after ensuring that they are indeed dealing with a potent batch.

Authenticity also matters when you are trying to find Peruvian Torch cacti with high mescaline concentrations. For example, the cacti that are sold in traditional Peruvian Shaman's markets are typically more potent than those that you may stumble upon in other parts of the world (or what you may acquire from local dealers).

In some countries and jurisdictions, it's possible to cultivate your own Peruvian Torch cacti, as long as you present them as ornamental plants. You might even be able to get your very own live Peruvian Torch plant over the Internet. Remember that large orders of mescaline plants could make botanists or law enforcement agencies suspicious of your intent. If you want to grow your own cactus, it's wiser to get just one or two plants and patiently cultivate them in your own home.

To grow your own cactus in a pot, you first have to acquire a properly cut live columnar stem of the plant. Find a large pot and fill it with special cactus soil; it should contain 25% washed sand and 35% perlite. Avoid using ordinary potted plant soil because cacti tend to thrive while growing in soils that are similar to those found in desert areas. Many novice cactus cultivators are tempted to infuse the soil with a ton of nitrogen fertilizer, but this is a bad idea because the nutrients will end up destroying the cactus. Ensure that your pot has proper drainage because waterlogged soil can cause the cactus to rot from the root. You can then plant your cactus in the pot, ensuring that the base is buried deep enough for the cactus to stand up on its own without needing to be propped up.

The cactus will get used to its new environment, and it will gradually develop a new root system. For the first two to three weeks, avoid watering your Peruvian cactus. Remember that cacti are desert plants and they are highly adaptable in conditions with little water. However, as the cactus forms its roots, keep it away from direct sunlight, or sources of heat.

After the first month, your cactus should be strong enough

to survive harsh conditions, so to help it thrive, you can simulate desert conditions by putting it in direct sunlight for about five hours a day. You only have to water the cactus once a week during autumn and spring, four times a week during summer, and not at all during winter.

If you look after your Peruvian Torch cactus properly, in a few months, it will be big enough for you to harvest and consume. Remember that the older it gets, the more mescaline it develops.

Peruvian Torch can be eaten fresh or made into mescaline tea. It can also be dried and crushed into a powder, which can then be added to juices or smoothies to mask the bitter taste. Like other mescaline cacti, Peruvian Torch naturally induces nausea in most people, so before you take it, no matter the mode of ingestion, have a vomit bucket ready!

You have to be very careful when preparing raw Peruvian Torch. Cactus spines can be quite dangerous and getting pricked by one can result in a major swelling. When harvesting the cactus (or foraging for it), ensure you either wear protective gloves or you handle the cactus with tongs. Use a sharp knife to carefully cut off all the spines before slicing your Peruvian Torch and consuming it. As you do this, try to salvage as much of the deep green outer layer as you can because it's the part with the highest amount of mescaline.

5

SAN PEDRO CACTI

The San Pedro cactus is scientifically known as *Echinopsis pachanoi* or *Trichocereus pachanoi* (the genus name was changed from *Trichocereus* to *Echinopsis* after the naming system becomes more standardized, but both names are still acceptable in scientific literature). The cactus is native to South America. It is found in Bolivia, Ecuador, Chile, Argentina, and Peru. Today, it has spread across the world, and it can be found in almost all continents.

The San Pedro cactus has been used for more than 3,000 years as traditional medicine for both humans and live-stock. Like other mescaline cacti from the Americas, it was (and continues to be) used for religious divination. Archeologists who study the Moche Civilization (an ancient civilization that existed in modern-day Peru) have found evidence of extensive San Pedro cactus throughout the civilization.

"San Pedro" is Spanish for "Saint Peter." The cactus acquired this name from Spanish explorers and missionaries who introduced the catholic faith to much of South America. As we've mentioned in previous chapters, the Spaniards tried their best to suppress the use of mescaline in South America. However, they also spent quite a bit of time studying local botany, and after learning about the "divine" properties of the cactus, they named it "San Pedro" because Peter is the saint who's believed to hold the keys to heaven. The rationale for the name is that the cactus can make users "reach heaven" during their trips.

The San Pedro cactus has a long and narrow shape, just like the Peruvian Torch. Its color varies from light green to dark green. Younger cacti tend to be lighter, while older ones tend to be darker. The columns are usually anywhere between two and a half to six inches (six and fifteen centimeters) in diameter for the mature plants. Each column has six to eight ribs. The cactus usually grows from anywhere between ten to twenty feet (three to six meters).

You may have noticed that the above description of the San Pedro cactus is almost exactly the same one that we provided for the Peruvian Torch cactus in the previous chapter. That's no accident. Those two cacti have many similar physical attributes, and as a result, many people confuse the two. In fact, it's not uncommon for online cactus dealers and even physical botany shops to mislabel a San Pedro cactus as a Peruvian Torch or vice versa. What's more, most consumers don't even mind the confusion; if your aim is to trip on mescaline, either cactus would suffice.

That being said, it's important, for educational purposes,

for us to distinguish between the two. The easiest way to tell the difference between a San Pedro and a Peruvian Torch is to look at the spines along the column of the cactus. In both cases, the spines are located along the edge of the ribs, at a 0.4 to 0.8 inches (one to two centimeters) interval. However, on the San Pedro cactus, the spines cluster out of whitish patches or spots, and they are shorter than those found on the Peruvian Torch. The San Pedro spines only grow to a length of 0.8 inches (two centimeters), while those on the Peruvian Torch grow to a length of 1.6 inches (four centimeters).

The San Pedro cactus also tends to be narrower and taller than the Peruvian Torch. Because of its height, the San Pedro cactus has branches that are more arched than those of the Peruvian Torch. The San Pedro cactus usually has multiple branches that emerge from a common base. Smaller branches also tend to grow in place of broken branches. This, together with the fact that the cactus has a super-fast growth rate, makes it highly suitable for multiple regular harvests. Once you cut off a branch, a replacement branch will grow in its place in a matter of weeks.

San Pedro produces white flowers at the top of its stems. The flowers open at night and close during the day (this is an adaptation that allows the cactus to reproduce under desert conditions without withering due to direct sunlight). In well-established San cacti, the flowers can be quite large between seven and a half inches (nineteen centimeters) and nine and a half inches (twenty four centimeters).

They are also very fragrant, which is part of the reason why San Pedro cacti are sold as ornamental potted plants.

When the San Pedro cacti flowers are fertilized, they drop off and leave behind oblong-shaped dark green fruits. Out in nature, the fruits fall off and create new cacti, but in cultivated gardens, the fruits are harvested (they are richer in mescaline than the rest of the cactus).

Just like in the case of the Peruvian Torch, the mescaline concentration in San Pedro cacti varies greatly from one plant to the next. On average, the concentration of mescaline in San Pedro cacti tends to be lower than in Peruvian Torch cacti. That explains why Peruvian Torch is a more popular choice for those who cultivate mescaline cacti for commercial purposes. San Pedro grows relatively faster than Peruvian Torch, but with Peruvian Torch, growers have a better chance of ending up with a highly potent yield.

For an individual grower, the San Pedro may be a better choice than the Peruvian Torch. The tradeoff that you get from a fast-growing cactus makes up for the likelihood of ending up with cactus with a lower concentration of mescaline. After all, if the mescaline concentration is low, you can always increase the amount of the cactus that you consume to get the desired psychedelic effects.

Apart from mescaline, the San Pedro cactus also contains alkaloids such as hordenine, anhalonidine, tyramine, and anhalanine. Some of these alkaloids have psychoactive effects that serve to augment the effects of the mescaline in the plant. They, however, don't exist in high enough amounts to create a "non-authentic" mescaline trip.

Potted San Pedro cacti can be propagated from cuttings or grown from seeds. A column from a parent San Pedro cactus can be grown vertically in a pot, and under the right conditions, roots are formed beneath the soil. For those looking to grow San Pedro cactus in gardens or raised flower beds, the better option is to lay a long cactus column in a horizontal position on the soil. This increases the surface area for roots to form on the bottom surface of the cactus. After a while, sprouts start to grow on the old cactus stem, and you may end up with a whole cluster of San Pedro cacti.

The San Pedro cactus thrives under a wide range of climatic conditions, which means that it can grow pretty much anywhere, as long as the soil conditions are right. While most cacti are only adapted to desert conditions, the San Pedro originates from the Andes (which are covered with rainforests), so they do very well in the cold climate that characterizes most of the northern hemisphere. It can even thrive during the winter in sub-zero temperatures.

San Pedro is more resilient than most other cacti, but it still needs proper care to thrive. If you grow a potted San Pedro cactus in your home, the most important thing to remember is that overwatering it makes it more susceptible to fungal infections which can destroy it from the root. You can water it a couple of times a week during the hottest months, and a couple of times a month during the coldest months.

San Pedro is susceptible to sunburn, particularly in warm weather. If it's overexposed to direct sunlight, it turns yellow, and its mescaline content reduces significantly. If you are a grower, you would have to ensure that it gets some light for half of the day and some shade for the other half. Low levels of sunlight are also bad for the cactus because it tends to grow into a structurally weak plant if it doesn't get enough exposure. If the San Pedro stays in the dark for too long (particularly during winter), its stems will narrow, and it could collapse under its own weight when it starts to grow again in warmer months.

When consuming San Pedro cactus, one crucial thing to remember is that its mescaline concentration varies greatly. The potency of one cactus can be eight times higher than that of another cactus, even though they are of the same species. If you have no way to accurately determine the potency of a batch of San Pedro, you should start by taking a small threshold dose of about 3.5 ounces (a hundred grams) of fresh cactus or a quarter ounces (roughly eight grams) of dried cactus. You can then gauge the strength of this dose before tripping on a larger dose.

6

BOLIVIAN TORCH CACTI

As you might have guessed, the Bolivian Torch originates from Bolivia. The locals refer to it as "Achuma" or "Wachuma." Its scientific name is *Echinopsis lageniformis* (in modern binomial nomenclature) or *Trichocereus bridgesii* (in the old nomenclature).

Compared to peyote, San Pedro, and Peruvian Torch, the concentration of mescaline in Bolivian Torch is pretty low. The average concentration of mescaline in dried Bolivian Torch is 0.56%, while the average concentration of mescaline in dried San Pedro is 5%. Technically, that means that to get the same psychedelic effects, you would need to consume about ten times as much Bolivian Torch in terms of volume.

Upping the volume to get a higher dose from the Bolivian Torch is problematic for a number of reasons. First, consuming large amounts of cacti is difficult because of the horrible taste and the fact that cactus naturally causes nausea. The second problem is that secondary alkaloids are present in Bolivian cactus in concentrations that are almost at par with mescaline. The more Bolivian cactus you ingest, the more these secondary alkaloids build up. Some of the alkaloids have their own psychoactive effects, and because of the cumulative concentration, these effects become more pronounced. As a result, Bolivian Torch trips aren't considered to be pure mescaline trips.

When you trip on the Bolivian Torch, the effects you feel are a result of a cocktail of alkaloids. If you want to have a general psychedelic trip, Bolivian Torch is as good a cactus as any out there. However, if you are interested in a genuine mescaline trip, you are better off going with one of the other cacti that we have explored in previous chapters.

Bolivian Torch cacti are light green in color. They have columnar stems with four to eight ribs. The spines grow out of nodes along the edges of the ribs in groups of one to four. Spines of the Bolivian Torch are quite distinctive. Their colors range from eggshell to dark brown. They tend to be uneven in terms of length; one node can have short spines clustered together with longer ones.

Bolivian Torch cactus can grow to a height of up to seventeen feet (five meters). Unlike the other mescaline cacti we have looked at, its surface is not frosty; it's clear and bright. In fact, its coloration is an important distinguishing feature, and even untrained foragers can use this quality to tell it apart from Peruvian Torch and San Pedro. However, thicker specimens of the Bolivian Torch look very similar to the other cacti, and the color test can be misleading.

Bolivian Torch cacti come in many varieties (all varieties contain mescaline and other psychoactive compounds, so it doesn't matter which kind you get). The standard variety is plain and column-shaped, and they are mostly cultivated for their mescaline content. The "cristate" and the "monstrose" varieties are more physically attractive, and they are mostly cultivated as ornamental plants. The monstrose variety is also known as the "penis cactus" and it has short thick stems with diminished columnar characteristics. In fact, looking at it, it's difficult to tell that it belongs to the same species as the standard Bolivian Torch. The top part of its stem is smooth and rounded with no spines (hence the name penis cactus).

Bolivian Torch cactus is one of the easiest mescaline cacti to cultivate because it is uniquely resilient and adaptable. It has a higher resistance to drought conditions compared to Peruvian Torch and San Pedro. It can survive on very low amounts of water, so you can comfortably take care of it even if you are the kind of person who forgets to water your plants for days or weeks. You have to water the plant during summer, but as for the other seasons, you might get away with watering it just a couple of times a month.

This cactus can survive in very poor soils, but the roots need good drainage. You should also avoid placing it under direct sunlight all day long. It's better to plant it under shade or to place its pot near a window that gets sunlight for about half a day every day. Too much heat and light can cause the cactus to become dehydrated.

Unlike other cacti, Bolivian Torch is easy to grow from its seeds. The plant produces fragrant white flowers that turn into seed-bearing fruits. These seeds are collected, dried, and then grown in seedbeds under warm and dry conditions. The caveat with propagating Bolivian Torch from its seeds is that it takes between one and two years for the seedling to grow large enough to be transplanted.

To propagate Bolivian Torch seeds, you have to create a mixture of sand, organic matter and pumice in a seedbed or container, then sprinkle the seeds on the surface of the mixture. After spraying a little water to activate the seeds, cover them with plastic wrap to keep them warm, and ensure they have exposure to natural UV light. The seeds usually germinate between one and five weeks. Remove the plastic cover once the seeds germinate, and place a stone next to the stems of the young cacti to keep them erect. Water the seedlings every three to five days, for the next six months or so; after that, you can start a less rigorous watering schedule. As your seedlings grow, you need to watch out for moss and algae because they can overgrow the baby cacti and suffocate them.

The Bolivian Torch cactus can also be propagated from properly cut stems of a mature plant using the same technique as the San Pedro cactus that we discussed in the previous chapter. The seed propagation technique is more popular because it's easier to purchase seeds over the Internet than it is to buy an entire cactus stem. Another great thing to note about Bolivian Torch seeds is that they remain viable for up to ten years, so you can keep them for a long time before you have to plant them.

The disadvantage of cultivating the Bolivian Torch in the northern hemisphere is that it doesn't have as much tolerance for cold conditions as other cacti such as the San Pedro or the Peruvian Torch. It can tolerate mild frost conditions of up to twenty three degrees Farhrenheit (negative five degrees Celsius), but anything below that could kill the cactus. In the long term, it's recommended that the cactus should always stay at a temperature of above fifty degrees Fahrenheit (ten degrees Celsius). So, if you live in Europe, Canada, or the Northern States, it's advisable to keep your Bolivian Torch cacti indoors throughout winter.

Bolivian Torch cacti (both seedlings and mature plants) thrive in mineral soils but not so much in organic soils. So, no matter what stage of growth your cactus is in, avoid adding organic matter to the soil. Organic material could create a culture of algae and bacteria that could destroy the cactus. Instead, when you want to boost its growth, you should use liquid fertilizers or crushed mineral rocks.

Bolivian Torch cactus is perfect for grafting other mescaline cacti. Grafting involves adding a part of one plant (also called a scion or a bud) to a different well established and flourishing plant (also called a stock). The scion receives nutrients and structural support from the stock, and it is able to grow just as it would in grafting stock for other mescaline cacti. Because of its ability to survive harsh weather conditions, you can increase your yield of other cacti such as peyote, Peruvian Torch, and San Pedro by grafting their stems onto a Bolivian Torch base. Many people who use Bolivian Torch stock to graft Peruvian Torch and Peyote, and San Pedro scions have reported high yields in a relatively short time.

7

LESSER KNOWN MESCALINE CACTI

Apart from the four types of mescaline cacti that we have looked at so far, there are many lesser-known species of cacti that contain mescaline to varying degrees. Most of these species are in the same genus as peyote, San Pedro, Peruvian Torch, and Bolivian Torch cacti, meaning that they are closely related, not just genetically, but also when it comes to their chemical profiles.

The mescaline bearing cacti we will discuss in this chapter are less popular for a few possible reasons. The first reason is that the concentration of mescaline in these cacti might be too low to justify cultivation for mescaline extraction purposes. The second reason is the cactus contains a decent amount of mescaline, but that is overshadowed by other psychoactive chemicals, so users who ingest the cacti won't have a pure mescaline trip – in other words, people want to trip on a hallucinogenic that they understand, rather than a cocktail of compounds whose effects may be unpredictable. The third possible reason is that the cactus might be so rare and so hard to come by, that few people have had the chance to forage, cultivate, or distribute it. The fourth reason is that the cactus may contain mescaline along with substances that are known poison, so it would be dangerous to ingest it. Here are some of the less known mescaline cacti:

Lophophora Genus

Lophophora diffusa: This cactus is in the same genus as peyote (whose scientific name, as you might recall, is Lophophora williamsii). It has very low concentrations of mescaline compared to peyote. The fact that it physically resembles peyote, and grows in similar desert conditions as peyote, has earned it the name "false peyote." There are many disappointed foragers who have gone into the wild looking for peyote, found L. diffusa instead, eaten its buttons, and waited for a trip that never came. Pellotine is the alkaloid with the highest concentration in L. diffusa. It has a strong narcotic effect, but it's not as good a psychedelic as mescaline, so if you ingest it, you'll most likely end up on a very mild trip.

Echinopsis Genus

Echinopsis scopulicola: This cactus is native to Bolivia and it belongs to the same genus as the Bolivian, San Pedro, and Peruvian cacti that we have talked about. The species is rare, so until recently, there were no scientific studies to back the claims that it contains mescaline. A 2010 publication found that the cactus contains 0.82% mescaline (dry weight), which is quite remarkable, even when compared to the more popular mescaline cacti. The cacti are readily available in South America, but it's yet to be properly popularized in the rest of the world.

Echinopsis spachiana: This cactus also belongs to the same genus as the San Pedro as well as Bolivian and Peruvian Torch. It's native to several South American countries. It is such a beautiful plant, that it's commonly cultivated as an ornamental plant across the world. In fact, it's commonly known as the white Torch cactus or the golden Torch cactus. It has light brown spines that give the whole plant a golden hue when the sun hits it at the right angles, hence the name golden Torch. The name white Torch, on the other hand, comes from the giant beautiful white flower with a yellow center, which blooms in spring. It does contain significant amounts of mescaline, although the exact percentages aren't known. However, we know that the concentrations aren't high enough to warrant the cultivation of this cactus for mescaline extraction purposes (that, combined with the slow growth rate of the plant, has led psychonauts to focus on other cacti in the same genus).

Echinopsis macrogona: This cactus looks a lot like the others in its genus, except that its spines are significantly longer. It is native to Bolivia, and it is known to have very low concentrations of mescaline. Its mescaline content is estimated to be between 0.01% and 0.05% of its dry weight. This concentration is so low, that foraging or cultivating this cactus for mescaline would be a total waste of resources.

Echinopsis tacaquirensis: This cactus is native to Bolivia and contains trace amounts of mescaline. The concentrations of mescaline range from 0.005% to 0.025% of fresh weight mescaline. That means you would have to ingest unusually high amounts of the cactus, just to get a threshold dose of mescaline, which is not advisable.

Echinopsis terscheckii: This mescaline cactus is native to Argentina, and it is very common around the Los Cardones National park. It is commonly referred to as the Cardon Grande cactus, or the Argentine saguaro cactus. It is a very large plant, and it grows taller than almost every other cactus in the Echinopsis genus. When it's fresh, the cactus contains between 0.005% and 0.025% mescaline, and when it's dry, it contains 0.01% and 2.38% mescaline. Owing to its large size, a decent amount of mescaline can be extracted from a single stem, especially if you focus on collecting the deep green outer layers of the cactus and leaving behind the inner white layers (the outer layers have a higher concentration of mescaline). Still, the low concentration of mescaline per unit weight makes E. terscheckii unpopular with mescaline enthusiasts.

Echinopsis valida: This cactus is similar in many ways to the E. terscheckii species, and its mescaline concentrations are within similar ranges.

Opuntia genus

Some cacti from the Opuntia genus are known to have trace amounts of mescaline. They include the Opuntia acanthocarpa, Opuntia basilaris, Opuntia cylindrica, Opuntia echinocarpa, Opuntia spinosior, and many more species. Some of these cacti may be known by different scientific names because the newest naming system split them into several different genera.

The Opuntia basilaris is also known as the Beavertail cactus. It has flat wide stems that rise from the base – the stems look like wide thorny leaves. It is quite common in the North American continent, particularly in Mexico and the American Southwest. You can find it in the wild, in states including Nevada, Utah, Arizona, and California. It produces pink flowers in the spring. Its mescaline content is estimated at 0.01% dried weight.

Another common cactus in the Opuntia genus is the Opuntia ficus-indica. This is a very popular cactus in the American southwest, and it has several nicknames, including the mission cactus, the Indian fig cactus, the Tuna Barbary fig cactus, and the prickly pear. This cactus is believed to have originated from Hawaii, and it's currently found in almost all continents in the world. It contains trace amounts of mescaline, and you are unlikely to extract a decent dose of the psychedelic unless you are dealing with very big batches of the cactus. The ficus-indica is consumed as a vegetable in some parts of the world, which proves that it's not possible to trip on just a few ounces of its flesh.

Opuntia echinocarpa is also known as Cylindropuntia echinocarpa. It has several colloquial names, including Wiggins' cholla, the silver cholla, and the golden cholla. It's commonly found in Northwest Mexico and the south-western United States. The cactus is native to the Colorado and Mojave deserts. It's probably the shortest of all the mescaline cacti that we have looked at in this book.

It looks more like a prickly bush shrub than an actual cactus. Its stems are made of short cylindrical segments that are covered with spikes. Its mescaline content is estimated at about 0.01% of its dried weight, and it also contains other alkaloids that have psychoactive effects.

The Cylindropuntia spinosior cactus is commonly referred to as the spiny cholla, the cane cholla, or the walking stick cactus. It's native to the states of New Mexico and Arizona. Its mescaline content is so little that it's almost insignificant. You cannot get high on this cactus, no matter how much of it you consume.

Why you should stick with well known mescaline cacti

As you have seen so far in this chapter, the lesser-known mescaline cacti escape the attention of mescaline enthusiasts for a reason. The mescaline content in these cacti is either too little or too contaminated to produce any desirable psychedelic effects. You might be tempted to find alternative sources of mescaline so as to avoid the challenges that come with acquiring peyote, San Pedro, Peruvian Torch, or Bolivian Torch, however, with a few exceptions, exploring alternative cacti is not worth it. Unless you are an experienced botanist, you should stay with the main mescaline cacti. However, it's good to understand what else is out there so that you don't get scammed by unscrupulous dealers or online sellers of mescaline cacti.

8

MESCALINE EXTRACTION AND
PREPARATION TECHNIQUES

We should start by pointing out that there is no single right way to consume mescaline. As long as you have a general sense of the dosage you want to take, you can ingest your cactus directly, mix it with other foods or drinks, or process it to a more concentrated dose before ingesting it.

It's important to understand why preparation is necessary before ingesting mescaline cacti. Mescaline cacti are wild desert plants. Most of them have spines, and all of them taste terrible. You have to prepare your cactus so that you can have an easier time ingesting it, and so that you can enjoy a smooth mescaline trip.

If you are growing the cactus yourself, it's recommended to wait till the column-shaped cactus is at least two and a half feet before harvesting it to get the best mescaline content out of it. For peyote, we recommend buttons with a diameter of 0.8 inches (two centimeters) or higher. After harvesting your cactus by cutting it off near the root base, cut off the top five inches (twelve and a half centimetres) of your cactus and save it – the tip is a perfect "seedling" if you want to replant your cactus.

Peyote buttons are spineless so they can be eaten whole, but in the case of San Pedro, Peruvian Torch, and other cacti, you have to get rid of the spines before you even think about eating the cactus.

There's an art to removing spines from mescaline cacti. Once you have your cactus stem, you want to get rid of the spines and the notches from which they protrude, but you also want to save as much of the green layer at the edge of the ribs as you can because, as we have mentioned, it's the layer with the most mescaline. If you are cutting the cactus yourself, you should protect your hands with gardening gloves. Use a small paring knife to carefully cut off the notches. You can also try pulling off the spines one by one before carving around the notches, but that would probably take too much time.

How to prepare a fresh dose of Mescaline

First Method:

Let's assume that you have a column-shaped cactus stem, at least one foot in length, and you have already pulled out your spines as instructed above. The next step you need to take is to peel off the skin of the cactus. Cacti have a frosty skin and a waxy layer underneath, both of which needs to come off to expose the juice green layer that's rich in mescaline.

Cut your cactus lengthwise in between the ridges. Make sure your cuts are deep enough to reach the center of the core of the cactus stem. Your cactus may have anywhere between four and eight ridges; after cutting along the center of each depression, you'll end up with strips that are equal in number to your ridges. Peel the frosty skin off each strip, one by one. You can use your fingernails or a paring knife to remove the skin. After that, carefully remove the thin waxy layer. You need to be cautious at this point because you don't want to lose the rich green fleshy part of the cactus. The sharper your knife, the more efficiently you'll be able to carry out this step.

After peeling your cactus, you need to remove the inner core. The core doesn't have much mescaline, and it will only make it harder for you to ingest your mescaline. When you look at the cross-section of your cactus strips, the distinction between the core and the fleshy layer should be clear. The core will appear "woody" while the flesh will appear succulent. Cut off the inner part of each strip lengthwise along the border between the core and the flesh. Removing the core is optional; you can leave it on if you want to minimize your wastage. After that, dice your cactus strips into chunks and eat them raw. You can also process your chunks further using methods that we will discuss later in this chapter.

Second method:

In this method, you start by slicing your cactus along the cross-section as you would do with a cucumber, producing discs that are about one-eighth inches (one-third centimeters) thick. Once you have your evenly sliced disks, you can remove the skin from each one of them (this should be easy because the slices are fairly thin. Start off at any point along the circumference of each slice, and work your way all around, following the curves of the ridges. Like in the first method, these slices can be eaten raw or processed further using more advanced techniques. If you plan on ingesting the cacti directly, you can eat the fleshy part and toss the core away, or you can eat the core too (although you should be prepared for a tough time chewing and swallowing it).

How to prepare mescaline tea from fresh cactus using the filter cloth method

This is a very simple preparation technique that anyone can do pretty well on their first try. It's easier to consume mescaline tea than to ingest raw cactus, so this preparation method is recommended for beginners.

In this method, you will need a blender, a large cooking pot, preferably one that can hold close to two and a half gallons of liquid (around nine to ten liters), a clean lint-free cloth, a wooden spoon, and of course, a one-foot long San Pedro or Peruvian Torch cactus.

First, you have to slice your cactus using one of the two methods that we have discussed so far. You want to have pieces that are small enough to fit in a blender, so if you are cutting the cactus into disks, you'll have to slice the discs further. After slicing your cactus, load all of it into a blender (or a food processor), then add some water and blend it until you form a smooth puree. You don't want any lumps in your mixture because it will take longer for you to boil it at a later stage. For best blending results, maintain the ratio of water to cactus at one to one (meaning that for every cup of cactus, add one cup of water).

Some experienced mescaline tea brewers dice and blend their mescaline cacti without removing the spines or skin because they don't believe in wasting any bit of the cactus, however, this isn't necessary if you have sufficient mescaline.

After you are satisfied with the consistency of your blended cactus, pour it into the large cooking pot and then put it on a stove. Slowly cook the mixture on very low heat. You really don't want to rush through this stage because if you do, you will end up wasting a lot of good mescaline. As the water-cactus mixture cooks, mescaline is removed from the cactus pulp and it is dissolved in the water, along with other soluble substances.

As the temperature rises in the cooking pot, the pulp will separate from the water, and it will float on the surface and form a substantial amount of froth. That's why it's important to use a big pot so that nothing boils over. Even with a big pot, you still need to keep an eye on the mixture at least for the first hour of cooking because the gooey green foam on top is likely to spill a little bit. Avoid covering the pot with a lid because that too will increase the likelihood of spillages.

After the mixture has been cooking for about thirty minutes to one hour, the pulp on the surface will start mixing with the water again, and the foam will disappear into the liquid. At this point, you will know that your concoction is no longer likely to spill. You can now turn up the heat and let the liquid in the pot boil over and reduce.

In most cases, you would have to cook your mixture for two to four hours. You will know that you are done cooking when only one fiftieth of the volume you started with is left in your cooking pan. Your mixture should now look like a dark, slimy, viscous liquid. If after the allotted time, you still haven't achieved the right volume and consistency, don't worry about it; just keep boiling it until you do. However, when you do this, you have to continuously stir the concoction to keep it from sticking to the bottom of the pan. If you neglect it, it will start to solidify and it may even burn.

After you are done cooking, take a clean piece of cloth and put it over a jug so that it serves as a fine filter. Pour the mixture from the pot into the jug through the cloth. You have to do this as slowly as you can. You can even do it in bits to give the mixture ample time to drip through the cloth. Once you've poured the entire mixture into the cloth, tie the cloth at the top with a string.

You want to be able to suspend it in the air for a while as you let the mixture drip into the jug or a collecting container of your choosing. There are many ways to do this. You can hold up the cloth the entire time, tie it to an overhead hook, or even tie it to a cooking stick over the jug; it doesn't matter, as long as you allow gravity to do its magic by dragging the drops of mescaline water through the cloth and into your container.

Let the mixture drip for about fifteen minutes, or until it

cools down enough for you to handle it. After that, you can just squeeze whatever liquid is left in the cloth out into the jug with your bare hands (ensure they are clean).

After that is done, you'll have all your liquid in a jug, and pulp in a cloth. Let the liquid cool down completely, and then pour it into a cup. Your mescaline tea is ready to drink.

Remember that even though the tea is easier to ingest compared to raw cactus, it is still quite bitter, and you might want to balance out the taste using various techniques. Some people choose to take the mescaline tea in a few quick gulps. Some choose to mix it with some orange juice to conceal the horrible taste. Still, others choose to squeeze in some lemon juice and zest and sip at the concoction until it's all gone. You can try one of these techniques, or you can come up with your own new technique; the important thing is to get the mescaline in your system to start your trip.

As a precaution, it's important to note that there is no way to determine the exact mescaline content in your tea. The potency of the tea depends on the potency of the cactus that you used in the first place. If you have no idea how much mescaline is in your tea, you should start out by ingesting a small amount, then you can top up your dosage during later trips after you have a sense of how much mescaline you are dealing with.

How to extract pure mescaline from dried Peyote, San Pedro, or Peruvian Torch cactus

We will outline a technique that you can use to extract

pure mescaline from a cactus plant. However, before we do, it's important to note that this process involves a bit of chemistry, and advanced knowledge of the subject may come in handy in this situation. Still, we are making the instructions as clear as possible so that even someone with basic chemistry knowledge should be able to follow the steps. The agents and reagents used in this process are readily available – they are not controlled substances, so you don't have to worry about triggering alarms when you purchase them from your nearest chemistry shop. However, you should take all the necessary precautions so as not to end up in any legal trouble.

You will need: a food processor, a stainless steel pressure cooker, a large stainless steel saucepan, distilled water, sodium hydroxide, a separating funnel (optional), benzene, sulphuric acid, pH paper, activated charcoal, filter papers (or coffee filters), and activated charcoal, ammonia solution.

First, you need two and a quarter pounds (about one kilo) of dried peyote buttons. Of course, you can substitute it with San Pedro or Peruvian Torch, but you should be prepared for a lower yield of pure mescaline at the end of the process. Still, it may be advantageous to use San Pedro and Peruvian Torch because they cost less compared to peyote.

Take your dried mescaline and grind. You can use a food processor, spice grinder, or any other appliance that fits the bill. If you have none of those things, a good old mortar and pestle would suffice.

Collect all your powdered mescaline and put it in a stainless steel pressure cooker. This part is very important – do not substitute the stainless steel cooker for one made of aluminum. In fact, do not use any aluminum cookware at any point during this process; aluminum is a light metal, and it's highly likely to cause a chemical reaction that will destroy your mescaline. Cover your powdered cactus with distilled water, seal the pressure cooker, and let it boil for thirty minutes. Strain the liquid and save it in a clean container.

You should not toss out your pulp after you boil it for the first time. A lot of mescaline is usually trapped in dried cactus even after boiling it, so you have to repeat the above steps several times to salvage as much mescaline as possible. After straining the pulp, return it to your pressure cooker, add the same amount of water, boil it for the same amount of time as before, strain it and save the liquid. Then do it all over again.

You should repeat the process at least five times. You can tell if all the mescaline is extracted from the pulp if it no longer has a bitter taste. After you are satisfied that you have removed all the mescaline you wanted, you can toss out the pulp.

Put all the liquid you have collected in a big stainless steel saucepan, and then boil it while leaving the pan open. You want to reduce the water in the pan as much as possible so that you have a thick concentrated cream.

When you only have one quart of the liquid left, turn off the heat. Weigh out 14.11 ounces (400 grams) of sodium hydroxide and start to add it to your mixture slowly, as you stir the pot. A chemical reaction will occur, and the outcome will be that the mescaline will be less soluble in water, and more soluble in benzene. If you have access to a large separating funnel, pour your solution into the funnel, and add 0.42 gallons (1.6 liters) of benzene. If you can't get a separating funnel, no worries; you can attach a siphon to a transparent one-gallon jug (about four litres), and it will work just fine.

After mixing the solution with benzene, shake it thoroughly for at least five minutes in order to get it all to emulsify. After that, let the mixture sit for two hours so that the layers can separate. After the waiting period, you will be able to see three distinct layers in your funnel or jug. Water is denser than benzene, so it will be at the bottom. Benzene will be at the top. In the middle, there will be a thin emulsion layer that contains both water and benzene.

If you are using a separating funnel, drain off the water at the bottom, and the emulsion layer so that you are left with the benzene in the flask. If you are using the jug and siphon combination, you'll have to carefully siphon off the benzene layer, and leave the water and emulsion layers in the jug. You have to be extremely cautious to make sure that the water and the emulsion layer don't get into your benzene. If any water or emulsion gets in, you'll have to repeat the whole process from the point where you add the mixture to the jug or separator and shake it. Accuracy is very vital here. Put your benzene aside in a container with a tight lid, or chemistry glassware that can be stoppered. Save the water and emulsion in a separate container.

When you have your benzene, prepare a solution of two parts sulphuric acid and one part water (you want to add the acid to the water, and not the other way around to avoid spattering). When your solution is ready, add twenty five drops to the benzene. You have to do it one drop at a time. After that, cover the benzene tightly and shake it thoroughly for one minute. Let it stand for five minutes. You will start to notice white streaks forming in the liquid and dropping to the bottom of the container. This is the precipitation of mescaline sulfates. If the mescaline cactus you used had a low concentration of mescaline, you would have to shake the benzene-acid mixture for longer to achieve precipitation.

After the streaks form, add another twenty five drops of acid to the mixture, shake it well, and let it sit for ten minutes. After that, add another fifteen drops and this time, shake it, let it sit for fifteen minutes. In the next round, add ten drops of the acid solution, shake, and let it sit for thirty minutes. Use pH paper to test the acidity of your benzene solution. Stop adding acid when you detect a pH of between 7.5 and 8. You can then let the precipitation go on until the process is complete. This could take several hours. In the end, you should have a clear liquid with white powdery crystals at the base of the container. Siphon off the benzene, and leave the precipitated crystals undisturbed.

Now, you want to salvage any mescaline left in the water and emulsion in the other container. Take the siphoned benzene and add it to the container, shake it well for five minutes, and let it sit for two hours. Separate the benzene and the two other layers again. Collect the benzene, and add acid solution, just like you did before. You can repeat these stages a few times to make sure that you don't leave any mescaline in the water.

After all that, you would then have to remove the little amount of benzene from your mescaline sulfate crystals. Use filter paper (or even the kind you use in a coffee maker) to filter the benzene so that your precipitated crystals remain in the paper. Then, wash the crystals by pouring ether over them and letting it drain until the crystals are dry.

Alternatively, you can put the benzene and precipitated crystals in a beaker, and then place the beaker over a hot water bath until all the benzene evaporates and dry mescaline crystals are left behind.

Now, you have mescaline sulfate crystals. You want to purify them to get rid of any contaminants. Dissolve the crystals in six and three quarter's ounces (twenty two mililiters) of distilled water at 195 degrees Fahrenheit (ninety degrees Celsius). Add a little activated charcoal to the solution, and filter it again, this time using the finest filter paper you can find. Collect the distilled water. Pour some more hot water through the same funnel to salvage any mescaline that may have saturated the filter paper.

Add a few drops of ammonia solution (10%) to the filtered water while it's still hot. Do another pH test, and keep adding the ammonia solution until your water has a pH of between 6.5 and seven.

Boil the water (preferably in a beaker to prevent any new contamination), until you only have two and a half ounces (seventy four mililiters) left. Let the remaining solution cool to room temperature, and then put it in a freezer or fridge, until it's very close to freezing. Crystals will form in the liquid. Pour the liquid through another filter. Mescaline sulfate is insoluble at low temperature (near freezing point) so the crystals will be left behind as the water goes through the filter. Put some ice water in the beaker, stir it a bit, and pour the water over the crystals in the filter.

If you follow the above instructions precisely, in the end, you will have pure white mescaline sulfate crystals with no contaminants at all. With these crystals, you can weigh out the exact dosage you want, dilute it in a little water or juice, and trip on mescaline, without having to deal with the awful taste of raw cactus or mescaline tea.

9

MESCALINE EFFECTS FROM A SCIENTIFIC PERSPECTIVE

In this chapter, we seek to understand how mescaline gets you high. We look at the scientific processes that are involved, starting with what happens when you ingest mescaline, going through how its metabolized and how it enters your system, then a discussion of what happens when it gets to your brain, and some general physiological reactions that might result during the various stages of this process.

How mescaline is digested and metabolized in the human body

Like every other substance that you ingest, mescaline is absorbed into the bloodstream through the walls of the digestive system (mostly in the stomach). Liquids start getting absorbed the minute they get to the stomach, while solids have to be broken down some more before they can get through to the bloodstream. This means that if you consume mescaline in solid form (i.e. raw cactus), it would take longer for it to get to your bloodstream than if you would have taken it in liquid form (i.e. mescaline tea).

Because of this principle, you can shorten your come-up time by "digesting" your mescaline before you even ingest it. First, you can turn it into a liquid or crush it into a powder. Secondly, you can add citric acid (lemon or lime juice) to it, and this can break down the mescaline right there in your cup so that it absorbs even quicker when you ingest it.

Food typically stays in your stomach for about two and a half hours before it starts to get released to the small intestines. Compared to the stomach, your small intestines are better optimized for the absorption of digested food. So, even though you will start to feel the effects of mescaline less than an hour after you ingest it, your peak is likely to happen two and a half to three hours into the trip, which is when the stomach opens, the mescaline hits the small intestines, and absorption fully occurs. Remember that the release of food from the stomach doesn't happen instantaneously; it's a slow process that could take a couple of hours or more. These two hours often coincide with the peak that you experience in the middle of your mescaline trip. After all, the mescaline has left the stomach, the concentration of the substance in your bloodstream will start to decline because there is no more incoming mescaline for the small intestines to absorb.

Most of the mescaline is absorbed by the small intestines. By the time the ingested material gets to the large intestines, the concentration of mescaline in it should be pretty low. It takes between five and twelve hours for ingested material to get to the large intestines.

If you ingest mescaline in liquid form, the time frame would be on the lower end of the five to twelve-hour range. The mescaline will be absorbed along with the water extremely quickly in the large intestine, and it will all be done by the seventh hour. If on the other hand, you ingest mescaline in solid form, it would move slowly, and the time frame would be closer to twelve hours. That explains why you can shorten the duration of your entire trip just by turning your cactus into mescaline tea. With liquid mescaline, you have a short intense trip, and with solid peyote, you have a lengthy tempered trip. It's up to you to decide which one you want.

Scientific studies on the metabolism of mescaline show that some of it remains the same when taken into the body, while some of it is oxidized and "deaminated" (the process of removing an amine group from a chemical). We've mentioned before that mescaline is chemically referred to as 3-4-5-trimethoxyphenethylamine. Scientists studied urine collected from people who had ingested mescaline, and they determined that after the mescaline combined with liver proteins, a big percentage of it turned into 3-4-5-trimethoxyphenylacetic. Notice that the difference now is that the "amine" at the end of the name has changed to "acetic." In minor cases, the "amine" was replaced by benzoic acid.

The important thing to note is that those chemical changes don't fundamentally affect the psychoactive properties of the mescaline. Although there is no scientific consensus at the moment, there is overwhelming evidence that suggests that the mind-altering properties of mescaline stay intact even if the "amine" part of the chemical changes during metabolism. In any case, only a small fraction of the mescaline is broken down in the first place, so your body is still left with enough mescaline in its pure form to work with.

Mescaline in the brain

Your brain contains different kinds of receptors. Where mescaline is concerned, we will focus on the serotonin receptors. These specific types of receptors are made of special proteins and they have ion channels that are used in the transmission of messages in the brain. Serotonin receptors are spread all over the central nervous system. They act as intermediaries when it comes to the release of neurotransmitters and hormones in the brain.

As a result, serotonin receptors play a key role in many brain processes. They are involved in cognition processes, memory creation and storage, learning, sleeping, and the gag reflex (which is responsible for the feeling of nausea). They also have a role in your mood, and in feelings of anxiety and aggression.

Psychoactive compounds target your serotonin receptors. In fact, all mind-altering substances interact with serotonin receptors to cause the effects that they do. Mescaline is no exception.

Mescaline falls under a category of substances known as non-selective agonists. That means that it binds with any kind of serotonin receptor. However, studies have shown that the psychoactive effects of mescaline are only manifested when it binds to a specific type of serotonin receptor known as the 5-HT2 receptor.

Scientists are at a loss to explain what exactly happens after mescaline binds with the 5-HT2 receptor, which precipitates the psychedelic effects. The leading theory asserts that when the binding occurs, neurons in the prefrontal cortex become excited, so sensory stimuli that come into the brain at that time are slightly altered, and so we perceive everything as somewhat distorted or removed from what's normal. For example, if a neuron (brain cell) that is involved in processing a specific image that you are looking at is excited, your brain might just change the appearance of that image. There is also the effect where different stimuli are combined and interpreted as one as if the brain's "wires" are crossed. For example, you may have heard of people who "see music" when they are under the influence of high doses of mescaline or other psychedelics.

Scientists have also found out that hallucinogens such as mescaline change the internal cellular signals in the cortex of the brain. The exact nature or mechanism of that change cannot be accurately explained or even predicted. That explains why people under the influence of mescaline or other psychedelics have experiences that are totally different, with very few common threads.

Mescaline is considered a neurotoxin. That is a general term that refers to any substance that binds to receptors in the brain and alters the default functioning of the brain. Scientists have found that the neurotoxic effects of mescaline vary from one part of the brain to another. Although it's not proven, this could mean that certain senses are more adversely affected by mescaline than others.

Physiological reactions that result from mescaline use

Compared to psychedelics, mescaline is relatively mild. It's between 1,000 and 3,000 times less potent than acid (LSD), and it's about thirty times less potent than magic mushrooms (psilocybin). This makes mescaline objectively safer than other psychedelics because it would take a very large dose to cause adverse physiological reactions. That explains why you have never heard of someone overdosing on peyote or any other mescaline cactus.

Even then, mescaline still causes a myriad of physiological reactions when it's ingested. With mescaline in your system, you will experience an increased heart rate, a rise in your rate of perspiration, and a rise in internal body temperature (which often indicates increased activity in the liver). You will also experience dry mouth, slight dizziness, and your pupils will be dilated. Additionally, you will experience nausea and anxiety.

Unlike the psychoactive effects (which we will discuss in a later chapter), the physiological effects of mescaline are not subjective. They happen to everyone, including people who have a lot of experience taking psychedelics. So, no matter how many times you have taken mescaline before, when you do it again, you will still feel anxious and nauseated.

There are some other physiological reactions that may not be universal to all mescaline users. For example, some people experience muscle weakness, contraction of the bowels and the uterus, loss of coordination, and reflux disruption (the term reflux refers to the backward flow of fluids in the body through a valve that's supposed to open just one way). Muscle weakness and loss of coordination may occur but go unnoticed if one doesn't move around a lot during the trip. Similarly, reflux disruption could be stifled in some cases, so that you feel nauseated but you don't end up vomiting. You might be able to do this by reducing the volume of substances that you have to ingest without compromising the concentration of the dose you are taking (e.g. by turning your cactus into tea or crystals).

The physiological reactions of mescaline become more pronounced when you take higher doses of the hallucinogen. Studies show that with high doses of mescaline, the increased heart rate could turn into increased blood pressure (also known as hypertension). While this may not be a serious problem for young and healthy people, it could turn out to be extremely dangerous in people with underlying heart or metabolic issues.

Mescaline intoxication can be stopped or reduced by valium or chlorpromazine. These substances are commonly used to treat people with mental health disorders, but they may be administered to individuals who are having bad physiological reactions to psychedelics.

10

MESCALINE AND SPIRITUALITY

As you saw when we discussed the history of mescaline, the hallucinogenic has been used for millennia in spiritual ceremonies, and it is a core part of the whole Native American religious experience. Here we will look deeper into how mescaline is used for spiritual purposes, not just by members of Native American tribes, but also by everyone else who is looking for spiritual fulfillment, or who yearns to experience the mystical.

To fully understand mescaline and other psychedelics, it's not enough to just look at their effects through a purely scientific lens. There's a vast body of work out there that links psychedelic trips to religious experiences. Some people believe that in the height of a psychedelic trip, the veil that separates the physical universe from the spiritual one is torn, and you can then catch a glimpse of what lays beyond. This belief is up for debate, however, the fact that so many people who have tried psychedelics (including atheists and skeptics) find it hard to write off this idea. That's because people under the influence of high doses of mescaline and other psychedelics, experience things that cannot be explained by the rules of the physical universe.

Mescaline use in Shamanism

Shamanism is one of the oldest religions in the world. It existed in the Americas long before the first Europeans set foot in the new world. Historians have found evidence that Shamanism dates back at least 10,000 years, although there is a possibility that the religion has existed for an upwards of 20,000 years. It's older than Christianity, Buddhism, and Islam, and although it's not as popular, it's still practiced by between eight million and nine million people around the world today.

The first thing you need to understand about Shamanism is that the entire religion is built around psychedelic experiences. For thousands of years, Shamans have used mescaline and other psychedelics as a bridge between their world and the divine. Christian missionaries who came to South America starting in the seventeenth century dismissed Shaman religious practices as demonic. Similarly, western scientists in the eighteenth and nineteenth centuries dismissed the religion as the "madness of the savage."

Thankfully, current generations are more open-minded than that. Many people around the world are giving Shaman practices a second look. Instead of limiting themselves to the rigidity of the scientific method, they are taking a holistic approach in examining the mescaline induced spiritual experiences. Being open-minded is not about using science and logic to explain everything; it's about putting yourself in someone else's shoes, experiencing what they have experienced, and then arriving at your own conclusion.

As old as it is, Shamanism is one of the religions that's capturing the imagination of many young westerners. People from America and Europe are showing up in large numbers to Shaman and Native American ceremonies because they are looking for authentic mescaline experiences. It seems that some have in them spiritual voids they are hoping to fill. Of course, many are just curious; and that's a good thing too.

Native American peyote ceremonies

Like the Shamans, Native Americans still use mescaline (particulary peyote) as part of their religious practices today, and that too has attracted many curious westerners who are seeking to experience something authentically divine. We've already discussed the Native American Church and how peyote is considered a sacrament in that religion. Unlike Shamanism, the Native American Church isn't only centered on psychedelic plants like mescaline cacti. It's centered on nature.

One of the most central beliefs of the Native American Church (and all Native American tribes) is that all plants are sacred because they were created by the Great Spirit. They believe that people should use plants because they are gifts, but destroying plants and other aspects of the natural environment is sacrilegious. That is why native

American peyote ceremonies are centered on appreciating natural beauty and reconnecting with nature.

To Native Americans, the visions experienced during mescaline trips are a way to commune with the Great Spirit and the rest of the metaphysical universe. They believe that each person has different experiences during trips because the Great Spirit has a different message for every single person. In some cases, younger members of the Native American Church share their visions with the older members who then help them to interpret the meaning of the messages that have been relayed through those visions. Many people receive messages to spread peace, to help others, to protect the environment, and to take up healthy habits.

Native Americans also hold peyote healing ceremonies; beyond the visions and the messages from the Great Spirit, they believe that mescaline trips can result in healing. They are also very inclusive, and readily welcome non-members to these healing ceremonies.

Native American peyote ceremonies are elaborate events where groups of people partake in mescaline out in nature under the guidance of an experienced religious leader. These religious leaders are known as "roadmen" and they double as medicine men and traditional botanists. They know a lot about different psychedelic plants, what kind of dosages to administer, and how to keep mescaline trips from turning into bad trips.

A typical ceremony takes place inside a teepee tent in a safe place out in the wilderness. It involves anywhere from ten to thirty participants on average. The participants all sit around a fire in a perfect circle. There's usually a designated member of the tribe that's known as the fire keeper. This person is in charge of maintaining the fire – he makes sure that it keeps burning, but he also changes the way it burns during different stages of the ceremony as fire has a lot of spiritual significance in Native American culture. The fire is used to conjure the spirits of different birds and animals, which are believed to have powers.

Everyone in the group drinks a specially brewed peyote tea from a shared gourd. After that, the roadman leads the whole group as they chant in the native language. Like the fire, the chants also help to conjure up the spirits and the ancestors.

Most people will start to throw up within the first hour after drinking the brew, but the roadman and the other experienced members of the group guide the newcomers so that they feel comfortable and composed even as they vomit.

Afterward, when the mescaline kicks in, everyone would have their own visions. However, since these are group trips, sometimes people have shared experiences. For example, some people have reported seeing the faces of the people sitting next to them morph into the faces of their own ancestors, or other spirits that have messages for them. For several hours, everyone gets to have their own trips as the roadman offers guidance to anyone who needs it.

Halfway through the trip, the whole group moves from the

teepee into a sweat lodge. The sweat lodge is hot, humid, and dark. Here, the natives chant even more intensely, and participants get to experience more visions and revelations. When everyone starts to come down, the group meets again in the teepee where they share some of their experiences, and the roadman offers interpretations of visions and some spiritual advice.

Not all mescaline users get to take part in Shamanic or Native American religious rituals, but that doesn't mean that they can't experience deeply spiritual mescaline trips. Sure, ritualistic ceremonies can enhance your trip, but if you can't go to one, you can learn as much as possible about them and try to replicate the processes even if you are tripping alone.

How mescaline might benefit you spiritually

By now, you understand that mescaline holds a lot of spiritual significance for Native Americans and Shamans, but the question remains: can it help you in your spiritual journey? To begin with, spirituality means different things to different people. Some people believe spirituality is about connecting with the mystical, and understand whatever is beyond this realm. Others believe spirituality is about finding something inside themselves that gives their lives more meaning, beyond the mundanity of everyday existence. Either way, spirituality is something that we all pursue, whether or not we consider ourselves religious.

Mescaline can be used in spiritual pursuits. It's highly suitable for this because it's a natural psychedelic. Many people who use it have experienced profound mysticism.

Some have been able to see the world around them in ways they never did before. Some have been able to discover things about themselves and to resolve internal conflicts in the wake of mescaline trips. You too can experience the same.

People who trip on mescaline often report experiencing a sense of unity with all things. They feel like they are one with the universe, like they are linked to all things, both living and nonliving, and they are just a small part of what seems like a vast infinite entity. The idea that we are a part of something bigger is a central tenet of almost every religion out there. Those who go into mescaline trips believing this almost always comes out with their beliefs affirmed. Those who go in doubting it, often come out believing it at least to some extent.

Many people who trip on mescaline also report feeling as though they transcend time and space. Some experience time differently; it may stop, move in slow motion, or move at a very fast rate. In other words, time is not as rigid during a mescaline trip as it is in normal life. It also can't be as easily defined. Some people feel like they have dominion over the space. Like they can move through space as though they are not limited by their physical bodies. For the first time, they get a true sense of just how unlimited the universe is. The sense that you can transcend space and time is a profoundly spiritual one because, at that moment, you realize that the physical dimension is just a construct and that there's more in the universe than our regular experiences and perceptions.

We have studied many reports of people who have tripped

on mescaline, and we have observed that many of them believe that mescaline opens their eyes to the true nature of reality. It's not uncommon for people tripping on mescaline to observe that things around them are fuller of life than they seem when they aren't under the influence of psychedelics. When you are on a high dose of mescaline, inanimate objects seem to be alive, and plants seem to have similar abilities as animals or even humans. Many mescaline users take this as an insight into the real hidden nature of things; like a spiritual revelation that helps them understand the truth that's hidden in plain sight.

The ineffable experiences of those who trip on mescaline serve as the strongest evidence of its spiritual powers. Many who trip on mescaline have heard, felt, seen, or otherwise experienced things that even they couldn't put into words. All religions describe the divine as something that's amazing, beyond human language or wildest imagination. When people tripping on mescaline have ineffable experiences, the kinds that can't be explained away by science, spirituality is the only explanation they can turn to.

The typical mescaline trip is characterized by lots of deep, positive emotions, which are an integral part of spiritual fulfillment. Apart from the initial feeling of nausea, most feelings that result from mescaline trips are positive. Overwhelmingly, people report experiencing feelings of peace, love, and joy when tripping. Their emotions are seen in many religious traditions as the "touch" of the divine in our lives. In rare cases, people experience negative emotions mostly as part of bad mescaline trips. Although these trips are rare, they too have some spiritual significance. They could mean that you are "fighting your inner demons" or that there is a battle between light (good) and darkness (evil) in your psyche.

Studies have shown that people who use psychedelics such as mescaline are more likely to endorse mystical beliefs, no matter their upbringing, level of education, or past religious convictions. Mescaline users are more likely to believe that they have a universal immortal soul. They are less likely to believe that death is something to be feared. They are more likely to believe that they are one with nature, the divine, or the universe. You could take the loyal atheist you can find, and once they have experienced a high-dose mescaline trip, it's highly likely that they'll admit to you that perhaps there's more out there than they initially thought.

When you trip on high doses of mescaline, you are more likely to make a distinction between your physical being and your consciousness. It's common for people to transcend their physical bodies while on mescaline; when this happens, they come to a realization that they only inhabit their bodies, and that their consciousness is who they really are. When your consciousness is detached from your body, it then becomes easy to understand why it's possible for you to exist in the form of a spirit. It starts to make sense that you may have existed long before you took your current physical form, and you may exist long after you leave it. In other words, you start to conceptualize the possibility of life before birth and after death (which, as you know, is a central tenet of almost every religion on earth).

One notable spiritual effect of mescaline is that those who use it regularly, tend to become less materialistic. The same is true for other psychedelics such as LSD and magic mushrooms, but it doesn't apply to all mind-altering substances. Some researchers have tried to understand this phenomenon, and what they have discovered is that when people experience "ego death" during psychedelic trips (where their minds feel detached from their physical bodies), they realize the futility of physical material attachments, and they decide that it's more beneficial to divert their focus towards things that truly matter (like positive emotions and charity).

People who trip on mescaline often report positive changes in how they perceive themselves, and they develop a newfound appreciation for life. These changes can be interpreted as spiritual nourishment or awakening.

11

MESCALINE AND PSYCHOLOGY

Research into the psychological effects of mind-altering substances was stifled in the turn of the century, but today, the world is more liberal, and there is a willingness both among the public and in the scientific community to take a deeper look into the benefits of these substances to the human mind. We are just beginning to understand how psychedelic drugs and mescaline, in particular, can be used to treat serious mental disorders as well as garden-variety psychological conditions.

Amidst the research into the psychological and psychiatric benefits of mescaline and other psychedelics, a new kind of intervention known as psychedelic therapy has emerged, and it's increasing in popularity.

Psychedelic therapy techniques were developed by testing the drugs first on animals. Researchers scanned animal brains and they were able to discover which parts were affected by which drugs. Through this process, they were also able to establish that controlled doses of psychedelic drugs did not cause any permanent harm to the brain, and they weren't inherently addictive either. With this discovery, the American Food and Drug Administration and governing authorities in other western countries started to allow limited use of psychedelics in therapy.

Mescaline use in psychedelic therapy

Psychedelic therapy utilizes psychedelic drugs that bind to serotonin receptors. These drugs include LSD, DMT, MDMA, psilocybin, and of course, mescaline. These drugs are selected mostly based on their availability and on the laws of the land, but mescaline has some inherent advantages over the other drugs in the group. Firstly, it's natural so it can be used without much need for rigorous procurement or governmental approval processes. Secondly, it's significantly less potent than some of the other drugs, so it's easier for the therapists to control the dosages offered to the patients.

Psychedelic therapy involves long sessions that start before the mescaline trip and end way after the trip. The patient has to be put in the right state of mind before they can even ingest the mescaline. The mescaline is then offered to the patient and once they are in a psychedelic state, they are subjected to an extensive therapy session. At the tail end of the trip, there is an additional session in which the therapist makes sure that the patient is able to relate the trip experiences to their real life, and particularly to the issue that they are trying to address.

You may have noticed based on the above description that the techniques used in psychedelic therapy aren't drastically different from those used by Native American healers. Basically, it seems that psychologists and psychiatrists are just rediscovering what native tribes have known for centuries; that mescaline and other psychedelics have the power to open up the mind in ways that nothing else can.

There is a growing body of evidence that shows that mescaline can be helpful to people with post-traumatic stress disorder (PTSD), obsessive-compulsive disorder (OCD), depression, alcoholism, and cluster headaches. However, the positive effects of mescaline in such cases are highly subjective; they mostly depend on the environment in which the mescaline is administered, and the accompanying support. That means that for psychedelic therapy to work, the subject has to be supervised by someone who knows what he is doing.

Mescaline and other psychedelics are increasingly being used to treat alcoholism. Some of these treatments are done in controlled trials. Most of the evidence of the effectiveness of mescaline is anecdotal, but there are a few science-based theories that could explain why mescaline might be helpful to an alcoholic.

The first theory asserts that mescaline can be a substitute for alcohol, and it can, therefore, make an alcoholic choose to trip rather than to drink. Since mescaline isn't anywhere as addictive or as harmful as alcohol, the shift from alcoholic dependency to period mescaline use then becomes a welcome improvement.

The second theory asserts that mescaline can help an alcoholic hit what can be referred to as a "simulated rock bottom." If you are familiar with the effects of alcoholism, you know that people addicted to alcohol find it hard to make drastic changes in their lives to curb their addiction unless they hit rock bottom. Hitting rock bottom helps many of them realize that drinking has completely damaged their lives, their relationships, their careers, etc. The problem here is that unless you are at rock bottom, it's difficult to picture what total misery looks like for you. However, mescaline can help you do that.

Psychedelic drugs can enable you to have vivid visions of what your life will be like if you lose everything. When you are at the height of a mescaline trip, a therapist can guide you and help you to picture what would happen if you let your alcohol addiction run rampant. You can see yourself lose everything without having to do it in actual life. It can dawn on you, that you are on the wrong path, and in the wake of your mescaline trip, you just might choose to go to your first AA meeting!

The third theory has to do with suggestibility. When we trip on mescaline and other psychedelics, we experience what is known as "ego reduction." Normally, we let our egos get in the way of us seeing the truth right in front of us, but when we are tripping, the ego is put aside and we are able to see things more objectively. So, if you are an alcoholic, chances are you will deny that fact or even react aggressively when someone points it out and outlines the evidence. However, when your ego is reduced, you will be more receptive when someone explains to you that your drinking is a real problem, and you are more likely to agree when someone suggests that you seek help.

Psychedelic therapy has become common in PTSD treatment in recent years. Most controlled experiments in this area are performed using MDMA, but mescaline has been shown to have similar effects and outcomes. In a recent study, two-thirds of PTSD patients who were subjected to several sessions of psychedelic-assisted psychotherapy were found to no longer have the disorder one year after the sessions were over. PTSD often doesn't respond to conventional treatment, and with an increasing number of veterans and accident survivors suffering from the condition, psychedelic therapy offers a great alternative.

Psychedelic therapy is also quite helpful to people who are terminally ill and are trying to cope with the anxiety that comes with facing one's mortality. It's hard to imagine, but when you are terminally ill, you experience debilitating depression and anxiety. No matter what system of belief you subscribe to, it's very difficult to wrap your head around the idea that you'll die soon.

We have mentioned in previous chapters that mescaline and other psychedelics can enable you to experience what's known as "ego death." This, as you might recall, is the feeling that your mind or soul is detached from your physical body and that you only exist as a spirit. That feeling can give you a bit of assurance and clarity when you are faced with your own mortality. That way, the anxiety and depression you are dealing with are somewhat reduced. Psychedelic therapy can also give you clarity about your personal values, and your life priorities. It can remind you that your life is intrinsically valuable and that you should cherish the things that you have accomplished, and try to get the best out of your remaining days.

Micro dosing on mescaline

Micro dosing is the practice of taking mind-altering substances in amounts that are below threshold (below the level needed to get you high) in order to get some mental or psychological benefits. People microdose on all kinds of substances. There's plenty of anecdotal evidence that shows that microdosing on psychedelics can improve a person's emotional balance, increase their energy levels throughout the day, increase their creativity and problem-solving abilities, reduce their depression and anxiety, and help them cope with addiction to other substances.

As we have mentioned before, mescaline cacti have lower potency relative to other psychedelics. This makes mescaline a great choice for those who want to microdose. An increasing number of people in Silicon Valley, Wall Street, and college campuses are taking microdoses of peyote and other mescaline cacti to give them a competitive edge in their studies and their work. Although there is no conclusive evidence that it works, those who microdose regularly swear by it.

It seems that micro-dosing works by rebalancing people by shifting their states of mind slightly and making both their physical bodies and their brains more attuned to what they need. The other possibility is that microdoses of mescaline have a placebo effect, and they merely give people the confidence boost to do things that they had the ability to do all along. In any case, many people report benefiting immensely from micro-dosing. We have come across a report from a young man who successfully used micro-dosing to regulate his severe stuttering. We have read about a student who swears that he was able to pass his advanced mathematics course because of micro-dosing. We have also come across numerous stories of young men who use micro-dosing to give them confidence in social situations (e.g. being able to approach and ask out women) and in career situations (e.g. being able to give presentations or speeches at work).

When you take a microdose of mescaline, you won't experience any serious visuals or auditory hallucinations, but you will notice slight changes from your baseline state. First, you will feel a slight stimulant effect; it will be as if your spirits are uplifted. Second, you will feel like a haze has been lifted from your brain, and you will be able to think more clearly. Thirdly, colors around you will be slightly more vibrant, meaning that you will be able to notice more details in your environment. In other words, a microdose of mescaline will make you more attentive, more observant, and more likely to engage your cognitive abilities. As a result, you will be in a better mood, and your performance of certain tasks could be improved.

Mescaline and positive psychology

Positive psychology is defined as the study of the good life. It's a branch of psychology that focuses on the positive experiences of human life, and on the well-being of individuals and society as a whole. Mescaline and other psychedelics have been studied for their positive psychological benefits, and their potential for improving individual lives and societies, in general, is immense.

Time and again, we have seen that mescaline causes behavioral changes that are beneficial to you and to the people around you. For example, it can make you less egocentric and more altruistic. Improvements in pro-social attitudes can make a person live a more fulfilling life. For example, if you donate to charity, treat others with kindness, and act less aggressively in social settings, you enrich those around you, but you also get the feeling of social acceptance in return. As a result, you are less likely to suffer from low self-esteem, anxiety, and other conditions that could impair your ability to be a functioning member of society.

Mescaline has also been shown to improve a person's well-being in a number of different ways. Scientists have noted improvements in moods, attitudes, and behaviors in people who tripped on mescaline. In effect, using mescaline might have the same positive psychological benefits that one might get from reading self-help books or listening to motivational speeches.

Using mescaline to improve your own mental health

Even though mescaline may be beneficial for your mental health, there aren't many therapists out there that are going to readily offer it to you as an intervention for mental issues that you may be dealing with. That's because, as a treatment, mescaline is still on the experimental stage and no professional is going to risk their license for you. So, if you are hoping to derive some mental health benefits from mescaline, you might have to come up with your own programs. We do not recommend substituting mescaline for your prescribed mental health medication. Always follow your doctors' advice above all else.

If you ever find yourself in a situation where you have to use mescaline for mental health purposes, there are a few things you need to keep in mind. First, make sure that you understand the dosage of the particular mescaline cactus that you are using. Know how much you need to take to attain a threshold dose, low dose, normal dose, high dose, or heroic dose. Secondly, you need to come up with a system that measures whether or not the mescaline is really helping your condition. For example, if you are using it to help your anxiety, come up with a series of questions that can help you measure whether your anxiety has reduced, increased, or stayed the same after your trip. Essentially, you will be performing some sort of psychological experiment on yourself.

After you have determined your dosage, and what it is you are trying to accomplish from your use of mescaline. You then have to get into the right set and setting before ingesting your mescaline. Set refers to your mindset at the time you take a psychedelic substance. Setting, on the other hand, refers to your surroundings prior to and throughout the duration of your trip. Since you are aiming for a specific effect, you need to find the right set and setting to increase the likelihood of attaining that exact effect.

For example, if you want to use mescaline to resolve certain internal conflicts that are causing anxiety in your life, you want to be in a mindset of relaxation and introspection before you take the mescaline. You also want to be in surroundings that are calming and secure so that you can focus on your internal conflicts during the trip. If you are anxious before the trip, it could backfire and you could have a bad trip that might cause more harm than good. Similarly, if you are in an environment that is unsafe and full of distractions, it could compound your nervousness and you wouldn't be able to get to the bottom of what's causing your anxiety.

When you are with a therapist or a traditional healer, they'll help get you in the right set and setting, but since you are on your own, you have to figure it out by yourself. If you are an outdoors person, tripping out in the wilderness could help you relax, but if you are an indoor person, you might feel more comfortable in familiar surroundings. Figuring out the right set and setting isn't that hard; you just have to know who you are and what will make you feel better.

12

OTHER BENEFITS OF TAKING MESCALINE

So far, we have looked at how mescaline can be beneficial for general spiritual and psychological purposes. In this chapter, let's look at some of the other benefits of mescaline.

Mescaline can be used to purge out negative emotions. In the practices of the Native American Church, purging is a crucial part of a standard peyote ceremony. Purging is both physical and symbolic. In most cases, it's done either by vomiting or just flatulence. In other cases, purging can involve crying, often loudly and violently, in a way that could disconcert any observer who doesn't know what's going on.

By design, purging has to be an uncomfortable process that involves a bit of catharsis. Purging has a cleansing effect on a person's psyche. It represents getting rid of old negative feelings and emotions and making room for new ones. We carry around a lot of negative emotions. We are angry at our parents, old friends, former lovers, and the whole world in general. We are afraid of our past catching up with us, and the uncertainty that our future may bring. All those things can weigh down on us, and make it hard for us to be the best versions of ourselves.

However, we can use mescaline to induce some sort of reckoning with that kind of emotional baggage so that we can experience them intensely all at once, and then let go of them. Mescaline can help you let go of anything that's burdening you and crippling you emotionally. All you have to do is focus on that one thing at the beginning of your trip, and meditate on it as much as possible throughout the trip.

Apart from purges, mescaline can also help you to experience a breakthrough on something upon which you have been stuck for some time. We all have moments in our lives where we feel stuck and incapable of making important decisions. You might be having a difficult time finding your passion, or choosing between equally promising career paths. You might be in a crossroads in your relationship, and you are having a difficult time deciding whether to end it or continue with it.

Many people have experienced breakthroughs over the course of a single mescaline trip. There are many reports out there about people who were unable to make pivotal life decisions, but then they went on "peyote quests" out in the wilderness, only to get back to their lives with clear decisions backed with strong personal convictions.

The most important thing to know about mescaline breakthroughs (and psychedelic breakthroughs in general) is that they can't be forced. They'll come to you naturally some-where in the course of your trip. You just have to trip in a place that is free from distraction, make sure that you take a high enough dose of mescaline, and try to think about your problem in abstract terms. There's no guarantee that you will experience the breakthrough on your first trip, so let things happen in their own time. At some point, when you least expect it, the answer to your problem might just emerge from your subconscious mind, and it will be clear as day.

Mescaline can help you to deal with loss or cope with bad news. When we lose someone we love, we go through certain stages of grief before we are able to accept what has happened and to live with it. For many of us, grieving can be difficult, more so if we are used to repressing our emotions, or if we are in deep shock. Mescaline has the effect of heightening one's emotions and bringing them to the surface, so you can express them properly. Beyond just coping with grief, mescaline can help us break down our denial mechanisms and give way to acceptance in many other areas of our lives.

Another benefit of mescaline is that it can help reduce self-destructive or suicidal thoughts. Researchers have found out that people who use peyote (and other psyche-delics) were less likely to harm themselves or to commit suicide than the general population. They were also much less likely to do it than people who used non-psychedelic drugs. The exact reason for this lower rate of suicide is yet to be established, but some have theorized that mescaline gives people a new lease on life, and they are able to see the world differently. This also relates back to the fact that mescaline reduces the rates of depression (as we discussed in the previous chapter).

There's also some evidence that shows that mescaline (peyote in particular) can make people care more about environmental conservation and the preservation of biodiversity. Studies conducted in the past couple of years have shown that people who used mescaline were more likely to take up environmentally friendly lifestyle choices such as vegetarianism, minimalism, recycling, and growing plants. That's partly because people who consume peyote often adopt the idea that we are one with nature, so they make real efforts to conserve the environment.

A surprising benefit of mescaline is that it makes you less likely to commit violent crimes. The US National Survey on Drugs carried out a study on the relationship between drug use and violent crimes. Now, this study was commissioned by people who were looking to prove that drugs are bad for society. However, when it came to mescaline and other psychedelics, they were surprised to find out that the exact opposite was true. It turns out that people who use mescaline are 18% less likely to get arrested for violent crimes compared to the average person. Additionally, they were 27% less likely to commit petty crimes such as theft.

Mescaline can help with our artistic ability. There are many accounts of painters and other kinds of artists who use peyote and other mescaline cacti for inspiration. Mescaline can expand your imagination beyond what you initially thought was possible. When you experience visions and hallucinations in your mescaline trip, you get to see the universe in a very different way, and that comes in handy in some creative pursuits. If you are an artist trying to paint a different world, a writer trying to describe a fantasy universe, or a composer trying to work out an original melody, mescaline might just be what you need to expand your creative abilities.

Mescaline has several medicinal benefits, but the evidence of such benefits is mostly anecdotal. Native Americans and Shamans have always considered peyote, Peruvian Torch, and San Pedro cactus as medicinal plants, and for centuries, they have used them to treat different conditions. Mescaline is believed to have the ability to treat fever, joint pain, and various types of headaches. There are lots of accounts out there praising the painkilling properties of mescaline. In fact, in some native tribes, mescaline is given to women during childbirth to help reduce labor pains.

There's also some anecdotal evidence that shows that mescaline might be helpful in accelerating the healing process for open wounds and fractured bones. Scientists haven't put much effort into studying the healing properties of mescaline, partly because most of the conditions that mescaline supposedly treats, already have functional medications that are accepted as industry standards. Specialists who perform pharmaceutical research only consider controlled substances after they have exhausted all other options.

That last benefit of mescaline, which is perhaps the most important one, is that it can make you happier. Happiness is not something that we think about that much. We go about our daily lives, and we rarely stop to take stock of whether or not we are happy. The fact is that our mood affects many other aspects of our lives. When we are happy, we become more productive, more creative, and we just enjoy life a lot more. As we discussed in a past chapter, mescaline works by activating serotonin receptors in your brain. The result is a positive impact on the neurotransmitters that affect how we perceive things, and how we feel about things. In other words, mescaline can put a positive spin on our feelings and perceptions, and make us generally happier people.

13

THE NEGATIVE EFFECTS OF MESCALINE AND KEY PRECAUTIONS THAT YOU NEED TO TAKE

Mescaline is still a drug and a controlled substance, and for that reason, it must have a dark side. It has effects that can be detrimental to one's health, wellbeing, and relationships. In this chapter, we will discuss the most common negative effects of mescaline, as well as the risks that are posed by the desirable mescaline effects. In each case, we will look at measures that you can take to protect yourself and those around you from the potential adverse outcomes that result from mescaline use. This information can come in handy if you experiment with mescaline yourself, or if you have someone in your life who does.

Negative outcomes of hallucinations

People do take mescaline for its psychoactive properties, so, arguably, the resultant hallucinogenic effects should be considered as positive reactions. However, the fact is that when we hallucinate, we do not have absolute control over our faculties. We can't always tell what is real and what isn't, and that alone puts us at risk.

The most common hallucinogenic effects are alteration in one's perceptions and sensory experiences. A person under the influence of mescaline might see colors and objects differently. He or she might also hear sounds that aren't there. In the height of a strong mescaline trip, vivid hallucinations aren't uncommon. One might also think that time is moving a lot faster or a lot slower than it actually is. Objects in one's environment might appear amorphous, like they have no distinct boundaries, and they just merge with everything else in the environment. One might see sounds and hear colors. One might feel as light as a feather, or as heavy as a boulder.

While these alterations in perception make for interesting experiences during a mescaline trip, they can put you in serious danger. Just picture this; you are in a public area while having the trip of your life. The sights and sounds are so vibrant that you can't tell them apart, but now you have to cross the street. First, you can't trust that you are reading the road signs correctly. Secondly, you can't trust your ability to contrast your walking pace against slow-moving cars in the street. Thirdly, you probably can't identify a car horn sound (if it's distorted) or even tell for sure if it's just in your head.

All these conditions create a recipe for disaster. Hallucinating out in the street can put your life in danger; you would be at a high risk of being run over by a car or a cyclist. So, it's better to trip in a safe area away from moving traffic (preferably in the safety of your home). Tripping out in nature may also reduce the risk of getting into an accident, but you have to be careful about where you choose to go. First, avoid areas in the wilderness with challenging terrain or dangerous wild animals (snakes, spiders, etc.).

For threshold and moderate dose trips of mescaline, it's unlikely that your judgment could be so impaired that it would put you and those around you at risk. However, as the dosage increases, so does the impairment. If you are taking a high or heroic dose of mescaline, you should take every possible precaution to keep yourself safe. This is especially important if you are an inexperienced mescaline user.

We highly recommend having a "trip buddy." Find someone you trust and have them watch over you to ensure your safety during the trip. Ideally, your trip buddy should be sober, but it's okay if he or she is tripping as well. Because people have different subjective experiences during their trips, it's unlikely that your trip buddy will have the same hallucinations and thoughts as you, and even though the both of you may have impaired judgments, by putting your heads together, you should be able to avert most problems.

As a point of caution, you should only trip alone on a high dose of mescaline when you are experienced enough to know for sure that you can handle it. We have come across stories of people tripping so hard on mescaline and other psychedelics that they want to walk through windows thinking that they are doors, and forgetting that they live in apartments that are several stories off the ground. This probably won't happen to you, but on the off chance that it does, it's better to have someone around to stop you.

Bad mescaline trips

Apart from altered perceptions putting you in physical danger, the hallucinogenic effects of mescaline can have negative outcomes when you experience a bad trip. The term "bad trip" refers to instances where hallucinations take a negative turn and they end up horrifying, traumatizing, or depressing you.

Bad trips often start with nervousness before or at the beginning of the trip. When you trip on mescaline (or other psychedelics), chances are that you are going to be nervous at the start. When your hallucinations start to kick in, they build on your prevailing state of mind. So, if you are nervous, you will interpret the visual and auditory hallucinations in a negative way, and that effect will compound, making you even more nervous. The same goes for other negative emotions such as anger, sadness, and depression.

Mescaline trips have an above-average chance of turning into bad trips because of the nausea it induces. When we discussed set and setting a couple of chapters ago, we mentioned that your environment and state of mind affects the nature of the trip you will have. Nausea often leads to vomiting, and both of these cause serious physical discomfort which can affect your state of mind. If you don't fight hard to stay composed through the first hour of your mescaline trip, there is a very high likelihood that your trip will turn into a bad trip.

To reduce the chances of having a bad mescaline trip, first and foremost, you should prepare for nausea and vomiting. Even though there is no guarantee that you will throw up, go into your trip assuming that it's an eventuality. If you are camping outside for your trip, identify an area away from your camping site where you will go to throw up. If you are tripping indoors, have a designated vomit bucket next to you the entire time, or ensure you set things up so that you have easy and immediate access to the bathroom when it comes to vomiting.

When you are physically and psychologically prepared to throw up, the anxiety around it dissipates, so it won't be at the forefront of your mind and it won't have as much of an impact on the nature of your trip. If and when the time comes to vomit, you just do it and get it over with.

You can also reduce your chances of having a bad trip by meditating. Our minds tend to run wild all the time, and this can be a real problem when a mind-altering substance is affecting our brain functions. We also have a natural tendency to dwell more on negative thoughts than positive ones, more so when we are anxious. When you meditate, you are basically emptying your mind, turning it into a blank slate. Those wild thoughts will go away, and you will calm down and have a pleasant trip.

Another way to prevent a bad trip is to work through any challenging turns that the trip may take. Minor challenges can turn into full-blown bad trips just because we are afraid to work through them. When a challenge presents itself at some point in the trip, chances are that you can tackle it head-on, resolve it, and go back to having a good trip. Just because it seems negative at the moment doesn't mean that you are locked into a bad trip for the remainder of the time. The reason bad trips escalate is that most of the time we try to avoid facing the problem.

To understand this point, picture this scenario: You see a door leading into a dark room. You can walk into the door and find out what's on the other side of it, or you can avoid it. If you walk in, you solve a mystery and you move on to something else. If you avoid going in, you will be running from it for your entire trip. Your mind might present a metaphorical scenario like this one because your subconscious is trying to work through something. The only way to stop the frightening thing is to confront it.

You can also prevent a bad trip by listening to soft music before the trip and during the come up. Soft, mellow music can put you in a good mood and reduce anxiety, so you won't be inclined to dwell on bad thoughts during the trip.

Negative physical effects of mescaline

Mescaline can cause tachycardia. This is a technical term that refers to a rapid heart rate, usually more than a hundred beats per minute. While this may not be a big issue in healthy individuals, it can be very serious to people with underlying cardiovascular conditions.

As a precaution, make sure that you are in perfect cardio-vascular health before you ingest mescaline. If you have a heart condition, do not under any circumstances, take mescaline (or other controlled substances for that matter) without explicit permission from your physician. A mescaline trip may be fun, but it's certainly not worth a heart attack.

Mescaline has negative effects on pregnant mothers and fetuses, so if you are expectant, avoid ingesting mescaline cacti (or other mind-altering substances). Research conducted by the National Institute of Drug Abuse shows that psychedelics negatively affect the development of fetuses, and they may lead to birth complications.

We mentioned some physical effects of mescaline when we covered the physiological reactions caused by the substance. Some of those effects are inherently negative, while others may turn out to be negative depending on the context. To recap, those effects include headaches, reduced motor function, and physical coordination, insomnia, reduced appetite, and flushed skin.

Interactions with other drugs and medications

There are no comprehensive studies that have been done to establish the effects that mescaline has when it interacts with prescription drugs. This means that combining mescaline and any medication poses an unverified risk to your health and wellbeing. When it comes to drug interaction, even if there is no conclusive information out there, it's always wise to assume that they'll be negative outcomes. So, by all means, avoid taking mescaline when you are on prescription drugs.

Despite the scarcity of information out there, we know for sure that mescaline binds to serotonin receptors in the brain, so it interacts negatively with medications that affect serotonin levels and those that are meant to treat mental conditions and disorders. So, if you are on antipsychotics, antidepressants, or even common attention-deficit drugs like Adderall, you should know that mescaline may counteract the effects of these medications, and it could make your condition worse.

Mescaline abuse, tolerance, and addiction

Abuse refers to the use of a substance in a way that causes harm to oneself or to others. Following that definition, it stands to reason that mescaline can be abused. If you take high doses of mescaline, you could cause physical harm to yourself. If you drive while tripping, you could cause an accident that could harm others. If you take mescaline while going to work, it could negatively affect your performance, your reputation, and therefore your career prospects.

Mescaline tolerance tends to develop very fast. When it comes to the topic of drugs, tolerance refers to a phenomenon where a person no longer gets the same desired effects from the same dose of a drug as he or she did in the past. The result is that the person needs a higher dose of the drug in order to get the same effect that he did before with a lower dosage.

If you go on back-to-back mescaline trips, you will develop a tolerance for the drug in just a few days. To avoid this, you have to take some time between subsequent mescaline trips, preferably seven to ten days. If you trip on mescaline for two consecutive days, you would have built a tolerance for the substance by the third day.

The encouraging thing about mescaline tolerance is that it's not permanent. So, once you stop using mescaline, your system will start to reset, and in the future, you will return to a baseline level of tolerance.

Mescaline is not physically addictive. When someone is physically addicted to a drug, they suffer withdrawal symptoms when their supply is cut off. However, with mescaline, even if you have been using it in high dosages and for a long time, when you stop, you won't have any physical withdrawal symptoms. So, technically speaking, it's not possible to be physically addicted to mescaline.

However, in the practical sense, addiction has both a physical and an emotional component to it. Even if you aren't physically dependent on mescaline, it's possible to be emotionally dependent on it. Mescaline can bring you many positive feelings and emotions. It can offer you an escape from the mundane aspects of your life. So, when its supply is cut off, negative emotions such as anxiety, stress, depression, and the feeling of vulnerability can take over, and as a result, you will feel a yearning for the substance. In this sense, you can be "emotionally addicted" to mescaline.

Compared to most other drugs (including other psychedelics), mescaline has a relatively lower abuse potential. Given the bad taste of all mescaline cacti and the lack of physical dependence potential, it's unlikely that you will ever find yourself needing to go to rehab to kick a mescaline habit.

14

MESCALINE TRIP REPORTS - MY SAN PEDRO MESCALINE TRIP

So far, we have discussed mescaline in theoretical terms; we have talked about its history, its science, its benefits, and its shortcomings. In this final chapter, we will recount the real-life experiences of people who have experimented with mescaline in two Mescaline Trip Reports. This will help you understand what it would really be like if you too tripped on mescaline. However, it's important to note that psychedelic trip experiences are highly subjective, and your trip might not turn out as the ones we are about to cover. These first-hand stories will teach you a lot about real-world mescaline experiences.

My San Pedro Mescaline Trip

My friend Dan and I have been experimenting with various psychedelics for a while now. We have tripped on DMT, Acid, and magic mushrooms in the past, so naturally, it was time to try out mescaline. When we decide to do something like this, we usually go all in. This is the story of our experience with mescaline, including both the preparation and the trip.

How we prepared our mescaline

We started with research, and we came across various preparation techniques that all seemed promising. However, in the end, we decided to devise our own technique, one that was loosely based on the pure mescaline extraction technique. We had a well thought out plan at the beginning, but as we went along, we had to make a bunch of educated guesses to get the whole thing to work.

I purchased 0.44 pounds (200 grams) of powdered San Pedro cactus from a guy on eBay. He came highly recommended from some of my other friends who had done mescaline, so I knew that his product was decent. We decided to trip on half the mescaline and save the other half for a later date. We weighed out half the powder, and then weighed that into two doses of 0.11 pounds (roughly fifty grams) each. We put each dose in a separate mason jar and added enough grain alcohol to cover the powder in each jar by about two inches. Our expectation was that the alcohol would dissolve the mescaline, and we would then filter it out, evaporate it, and we would be left with pure mescaline.

After mixing the grain alcohol and the mescaline, we were surprised to see the liquid turn to a dark green color, as much of the cactus powder settled at the bottom of the jar. We thought this was odd because we expected the mixture to form an emulsion. Dan suspected that we might have been scammed, but after doing a little more online research, we realized that this was a common occurrence, so it was completely normal.

We left the mixture in the jars for three days, only shaking it once in a while to agitate the liquid in order to increase the rate of dissolution. In this technique, we were supposed to strain the mixture, save the grain alcohol, and then re-submerge the mescaline powder and repeat the whole process two more times. This meant that it would take us nine whole days just to separate the mescaline from the cactus powder. At first, we were committed to doing it right, but after straining the mescaline for the first round, we grew impatient.

We both had coincidental off days coming up, and we figured that it would be the perfect D-day for our mescaline trip. Two days after straining the mescaline for the first time, we decided to do our second and last strain. We knew that we were leaving some mescaline on the metaphorical table, but it didn't matter; we just wanted to trip.

It was time to evaporate the mescaline-alcohol solution. We poured the solution collected from each Mason jar in separate Pyrex baking trays. We wanted the liquid to have as much surface area as possible to hasten the evaporation process. We put the baking trays on a table next to a large open window. We turned on two powerful fans to blow over the liquid, and we let the fans run overnight.

The next day, we were disappointed to find out that not much of the liquid had evaporated. That's when we decided to improvise. I brought the hairdryer from the bathroom, and Dan brought an electric heater. We directed as much hot air over the baking trays as we could. In about forty minutes, the liquid in one of the trays was mostly gone, leaving behind what looked like black tar. We narrowed down on the other tray, and before the hour was up, it too only had dark tar at the bottom.

We each scrapped the dark tar from the bottom of our respective baking dishes. It was quite sticky and annoying to handle. Dan suggested adding breadcrumbs to the tar to make it less sticky and then rolling it into a ball. He rolled his tar perfectly, and then he helped me out with mine.

When it was time to ingest the mescaline, we each cut up our balls of mescaline tar into small pieces, dipped the pieces in sugar, and then swallowed them with barely any chewing. The pieces of mescaline tar had a horrible after-taste, so we washed them down with orange juice. Compared to accounts of people eating raw cactus or drinking mescaline brew, I bet we had an easier time taking in our mescaline. The pieces of mescaline tar were all gone in less than a minute.

The trip

It was about 5 p.m. when we ingested the mescaline. I started to feel the effects of the mescaline within ten to twenty minutes after ingesting the ball of tar. Everything started to appear brighter, almost crisper. This caught me by surprise and I had to confirm with Dan that he too was starting to feel different. We had read that mescaline typically takes longer than that to kick in, so we speculated that we were dealing with some really good stuff.

Our come up was characterized by a strange silence. We had agreed to stay quiet and maybe meditate as the trip took off, but the silence started to feel sort of loud. It felt like I could hear the absence of sound!

Dan still had a bit of an appetite going, so he ate a piece of cold pizza from the fridge. This was a mistake that he regretted almost immediately. Just as he was finishing off the last bite, he realized that he was starting to feel sick. He fought off the urge to throw up, and he mentioned that he was developing a headache.

Dan's condition contrasted with mine. I was starting to feel happier and more energized, and I told him that I wished he was in the same headspace as I was. He decided to lay down on the bed for a while to see if things would change.

Half an hour after ingesting the mescaline, I felt like there was this boundless energy coursing through my entire body. The energy was all over, all at once; it was in my veins, my heart, my lungs, the pit of my stomach, and the top of my head. I felt like I was indestructible, like right there and then, I could turn into a superhero. Still, even with this boost of energy, I felt grounded, like all my senses were intact. I have been on other substances before and in those cases, feelings of energy surges in my body were accompanied by crazy urges to jump around, act in a rowdy manner, and maybe even punch someone in the face – this was different because I remained calm and rational.

Dan came back out of his bedroom less than ten minutes after he had left to lie down. He claimed that he was feeling slightly better, and he thought it would be a good idea to "walk-off" his bad reaction. We both went out and walked around a nearby senior community center. It was a beautiful place, with meandering trails and a nice laidback fountain.

At this point, things didn't look too removed from reality, but they were vibrant, and they just seemed more beautiful. As the path narrowed ahead of us, it felt as though we were walking through a paint; maybe an artistic depiction of the Garden of Eden. It also felt as though the hedges and the tree branches along the trail were staring at us.

I had a broad smile plastered on my face the entire time, and after a while, my facial muscle developed a slight ache. It wasn't particularly uncomfortable; it just felt like I was hyper-aware of muscle contractions in my jaws.

We met up with two girls from the neighborhood, and they joined us for the walk. They knew about our past experimentations with mind-altering substances, so we had told them that we were tripping on cactus that evening. They had a few follow-up questions, but they were basically cool with it. When we mentioned that we wanted to trip out in nature, they offered to show us a nearby wooded area along their usual jogging route that would be perfect for our trip. We all decided to go there together.

At this point, it was about an hour after we had taken the mescaline. The forest was breath-taking and beautiful. Unlike the trees in the community center, the ones in the forest were taller and majestic. When the sunlight hit the leaves, they seemed to pop like glitter against a dark green background.

We made our way up a jogging trail through the woods, and soon we found ourselves atop a hill. The sun was bright orange and it looked like it was hanging right above the ground far out on the horizon. It was just about it set, and it looked surreal. It showered the entire landscape with orange embers. We stood there for a while and just took it all in. It looked so awesome, I felt like I was going to cry.

After a while, we started walking again. We were conversing, mostly on topics about humanity, nature, and the universe. For the life of me, I can't remember much of what I said. What I do recall is that all the points I made were deeply philosophical and poetic. I've since asked Dan if he remembers much of what we said, but he doesn't either. His only recollection was that he talked so much between breaths that he developed a sore throat. Our two friends were a few paces behind us most of the time, and they were having a conversation of their own at this point.

An hour and a half, or maybe two hours into the trip, I could feel that I was having a full psychedelic body buzz. I felt way more confident than I usually do. Normally, I am very reserved in the company of ladies, and it makes me come off as a little shy. However, with the mescaline in full effect, I felt self-assured and I started showing off. My tone and general way of speaking had changed, and I remember thinking that I sounded classier.

For instance, at some point, we came across a large puddle of muddy water that blocked the entire trail. When one of the girls asked what we intended to do, I said: "We shall traverse, since the obstacle is, in fact, the path." I proceeded to jump over the entire puddle, and despite feeling a bit out of balance, I landed on the other side just fine. The others, inspired by me, followed suit with varying degrees of success (one of the girls almost made it over but she got the heel of her sneaker dirty).

After that, I felt so confident that I started walking around the darkening forest with my head held high, and without watching my step. I have dreamlike recollections of these moments, so one of the girls filled me in on some of the details. Apparently, I kept saying that I was totally sure of my position in the world and that I felt a deep connection to the earth below me, and for that reason, I was certain that I couldn't bump into anything, stumble, or even fall. The girl claims that my movement seemed staggered at the moment, but she concedes that I didn't stray from the trail or came close to falling despite the uneven terrain.

I remember turning my head up as we walked among the trees. My field of vision was only populated with tree branches and the twilight sky, so it felt to me like I was drifting through the forest, not walking. It was a lot of fun, just watching branches and leaves moving slowly past me. At some point, my mind got a little twisted, and it felt as if everything around was moving, and I was the one standing still.

Another thing I remember about this part of the trip is that Dan and I were laughing a lot. Everything anyone said sounded hilarious to me, and so I was bursting into laughter pretty much every other second. At times, I would start chuckling at some random idea that just popped into my head. Stray thoughts like "that tree branch looks kind of like an arm" would send me reeling with laughter, and the girls would start wondering what I was laughing about.

It was two and a half hours into the trip, and I started to feel different. My trip had been easy going so far, but suddenly, I felt like there was a shift in the nature of my body buzz, and it now felt too intense. It was a familiar feeling. At first, I couldn't place it, but in a few moments, I realized that feelings of nausea were creeping up.

I have had stomach ulcers for years, but in my research, I hadn't come across anything that suggested mescaline could make my condition worse. Now, I started to worry that I had made a terrible mistake. My stomach felt sensitive, and I had this scary picture in my head that the mescaline had punctured gaping holes along its lining, and that I might need serious medical attention.

As that scary thought became more vivid in my head, I got very sick, and I dashed to the side of the trail and threw up at the base of a mossy tree. I squatted there and heaved for several minutes, spewing weird green puke on the tree and the ground next to it. It had a watery consistency to it, and I figured it was because I had drunk a lot of orange juice with the mescaline earlier.

The girls kept their distance, but Dan walked over to assure me: "We knew this would totally happen so it's cool!" he said. It didn't help. As I was throwing up, I felt a piercing and burning sensation in my stomach, chest area, and throat.

After I was done throwing up. I felt quite relieved. It was like I had been carrying a heavy load with me all along without realizing it, and now that I had unloaded, I felt lighter, freer. I looked up at the sky. It was now metallic blue, and I know it would be dark soon. We all decided to go back home. We moved as fast as we could, and the walk was uneventful. The girls branched off when we got back to civilization, and Dan and I went back to our place.

When we got home, I felt a cold sweat coming on, and I thought that I should go and lay down for a second before I continued with any other plans for the evening.

The next thing I remember was sitting up in my bed with absolutely no idea where I was. It took me maybe a whole minute to figure out that I was in my room, then several other minutes to remember that I had, in fact, walked in there myself. I'm not even sure if I was napping. It's possible that I drifted off into deep thought and I just lost a sense of my surroundings. I had no idea what time it was. It was completely dark outside.

I went back to the living room and I found Dan getting his jacket, ready to go outside. He picked up his keys and told me he was going to meet his sister somewhere in town. It appeared he had sobered somewhat, and he felt okay to drive. Before leaving, he asked if I was feeling better, and for the first time, I realized that my cold chills had slightly subsided.

After Dan left, I wanted to eat something, but I feared that my nausea would come back, so I took some nausea medication instead. I tried watching TV, but nothing good was on.

On the couch, I found myself on a loop that was straight-up confusing. I would start nodding off, and I'd lean into it, closing my eyes and lying back. However, just a few seconds later I would wake up in a cold sweat and kick my limbs off like I was having a seizure. This happened several times, and it got to a point where I decided to force myself to just stay awake throughout.

I looked around the room and I noticed that the room was moving in the direction of my eyes. It seemed as though when I shifted my eyes, the whole room slightly shifted with them. It felt like I was viewing my whole reality through a window or a screen. Everything looked the same, and yet it all felt surreal. After a while, I found myself in a state where I couldn't tell if I was awake or dreaming. I think I was somewhere in between; in a sleep-wake limbo, if there is such a thing.

Occasionally, I would hear a small voice, each time seeming to come from a different part of the room. I wasn't sure if it was real or just in my head. I felt like it was trying to tell me something important, but just as I thought I was starting to make out the message, the voice would disappear. I had read stories about people on mescaline communicating with entities or spirits, but whatever that voice was, I didn't get anything it was saying.

Dan opened the door and walked back into the room. I barely noticed that he was back (or that there was someone entering the house) until he was standing right in front of me. For the life of me, I couldn't tell how long he had been gone. It might have been three minutes or three days; at that point, my mind could not keep track of time at all. In fact, I wasn't entirely sure if Dan was really back or if he was just a hallucination.

"I'm messed up!" I said to Dan.

Dan reminded me that I had been on worse trips before, and whatever I was dealing with, I could power through it. We sat on the couch and talked for a while, though I could barely keep track of the conversation.

At some point, I suddenly realized that all the negative energy in me had just dissipated. My cold sweats, drowsiness, and latent feelings of nausea were all gone. I think all the discomfort had just run its course, and it then gave way to a feeling of bliss. I felt more relaxed than I had ever been at any point in my life, and I just wanted to prolong that feeling and stay in that moment forever.

Still feeling great, I went to my bedroom, changed, and got into my warm bed. I cuddled with my large stuffed bear, smiling the whole time, and occasionally giggling like a little kid. After a while, I thought the bear's eyes were kind of creepy, so I tossed it to the floor. For the rest of my trip, I lay in bed, recounting the things that had happened that day.

My comedown was very blissful. There were times when I thought the mescaline had totally worn off, but then I'd notice some latent visuals. The next morning, things seemed brighter than usual, but by midday, they had completely returned to normal.

My Breakthrough Mescaline Trip Report

It all started around a quarter past ten on a Sunday morning. I had acquired a batch of bridgesii (Bolivian Torch) powder, and I planned on taking 0.7 ounces (twenty grams) for my trip. I was planning to ingest the mescaline at precisely 11 a.m., so with just forty-five minutes to go, I felt it was the right time to get myself ready. As a precautionary measure, I swallowed two anti-nausea pills, then sat back on the couch, relaxed, and listened to some music.

Soon it was 11 a.m., and I was ready to begin. I had already weighed out my dose of powdered mescaline and it was sitting in a small bowl on the coffee table. I scooped out a heaped tablespoon of powder and shoved it into my mouth. I had heard lots of stories about how bad the cactus tasted and I figured that I could take it as fast as possible just to get it over with – big mistake!

The horrible taste of the mescaline seemed to hit my senses all at once. I gagged and choked. I started coughing, spewing the powder out of my mouth and onto the table. I hurriedly chugged on some cooled down coffee that I had prepared for the purposes of washing down the mescaline. The coffee didn't help much, and I continued to dry heave for several minutes.

At a quarter past eleven, I had calmed down somewhat, so I decided to try a different approach. I stirred a few spoonfuls of the cactus powder into a mug of cold coffee and chugged it. This was better than my original plan, but inasmuch as the coffee helped the mescaline go down smoothly, it didn't do much to mask the bad taste. I decided to switch from coffee to orange juice instead. This time, it tasted just a little better, and by half-past eleven, I had managed to ingest all the mescaline powder.

About five minutes after swallowing my last gulp of mescaline-orange juice mixture, I was hit by a massive wave of nausea. It took all my strength and mental fortitude to keep the mescaline down. For the next quarter-hour or so, I was literally fighting my gag reflex, hoping that my system would absorb as much mescaline as possible before I lost the battle. I was leaning against the kitchen table when I finally gave in.

My stomach turned and I managed to grab an empty bowl just as the vomit came out. I threw up for about five minutes straight. When I was done, I found myself staring into a bowlful of disgusting green goop. Although I felt relieved physically, I knew that thus far, my mescaline trip plans weren't going so well.

I was determined to salvage my trip at any cost, so I did the craziest thing that I could at that moment. I chugged on my own puke! It was a spur of the moment decision that left me bewildered. It had a slimy texture and I felt like I was drinking a vat of mucus. The next thing I remember was dropping the empty bowl and rushing to the sink to wash out my mouth, thinking to myself "I can't believe I just did that!"

From my original batch, I had only a third of an ounce (about ten grams) left. After washing out my mouth I thought "Well this can't get any crazier," so I decided to ingest that amount too.

It was a few minutes past noon, and at the moment, I had roughly one ounce of mescaline cactus in my system. The nausea was acting up again, and this time, I knew there was no way in hell I'll be drinking puke again. I fought the urge to vomit the best I could, and when it was clear that I was in a losing battle, I ran to the bathroom and got there just in time to projectile vomit straight into the washbasin.

Once I was done purging, I felt totally empty and deeply relieved. The only discomfort I was experiencing at this point was a faint cramp in my stomach. This cramp would crop up once in a while during my entire trip, but it wasn't that much of a distraction, and at some point in the afternoon, I stopped noticing it altogether.

Heading back to the bathroom after the purge, I started to feel an intense body buzz coming on. It rose quite fast, which made it feel somewhat overwhelming.

It was half-past noon. I sat on my couch and put on some electronic music. I reclined the seat as far back as I could. I tried to relax and let the mescaline take me on a ride.

At about forty minutes past noon, I started to feel quite giddy. My body buzz was still there, but now it felt like my brain too was vibrating. It seemed like every nerve in my body had extra electric current charging through it, like I was a battery filled with power beyond my usual capacity. At 1 p.m., it was clear to me that even though I had thrown up, my body had retained enough mescaline, and I was having a full-blown trip. All that suffering and discomfort that I had gone through was not in vain.

From this point on, I cannot say with absolute certainty that the subsequent events happened in chronological order, and I cannot make an accurate estimate of the timing of each event. I've tried to recount them to the best of my recollection, but one of the first things you'll realize about mescaline is that it warps your sense of time.

At about a quarter past one, I realized that I was shivering. I decided to bundle up and cover myself with a light blanket. It was a very odd feeling – my shiver was juxtaposed with the feeling of total pleasure washing over my body.

Looking up at the ceiling, I noticed an intricate pattern of slow-moving shapes. They seemed to emerge from the square pattern on the boards, and then take a life of their own. I closed my eyes, and my visual field was instantly populated with structures that seemed to drift about aimlessly. The colors of the structures would change in a pulsating pattern. One moment, they were in black and white, and the next moment, they had all sorts of rainbow hues. They also changed from two-dimensional shapes to three-dimensional complex patterns, and then back again.

At roughly 2 p.m., I opened my eyes, got up from the couch, and walked into the dining area to get a glass of water off the dispenser. The action of walking felt oddly pleasurable to me. It seemed that with every step I took, a strangely awesome sensation would generate from the base of my foot and flow upwards through my body. I also noticed that my walk wasn't perfect and that I was a little out of balance.

There was a bouquet of flowers at the center of the table. All the flowers seemed to breathe in a perfectly synchronized rhythm. I thought it looked strange so I went in for a closer look. The colors were somewhat enhanced and the flowers were brighter. The petals were vibrating, and upon scrutiny, they seemed to be dancing to some inaudible beat. I busted out laughing at the thought that those stalks of flowers were better dancers than I was.

I went back to the couch, grabbing my acoustic guitar along the way. I started playing it. It felt very odd. The fretboard appeared a lot shorter than it normally does. I strummed a few of my favorite songs, but I couldn't seem to create anything remotely melodic; it seemed that thanks to the mescaline, my skill levels had significantly dropped. Still, the feel and the vibration of the guitar strings gave me a lot of pleasure, so I kept playing.

At about quarter to three, I put my guitar aside and sat down on my rug. The rug felt awesome against my skin like it was tickling every inch of my body. I decided to lay on the rug and roll around like a worm. It was great; I felt like every cell in my body was experiencing peak levels of pleasure.

Sometime around 3 p.m., I started to have long introspective thoughts about my life. I looked at my life and took stock of what I had accomplished so far. My thoughts quickly drifted to some unpleasant childhood memories, the kind that got stuck in my psyche and affected my confidence as an adult. At this point, I was lying on the carpet, and I started to feel like it was moving beneath me. I decided to pay no attention to my hallucinations, and instead, to focus on my unresolved personal issues.

All the dark things about me came to the surface, all at the same time. I thought about my repressed memories and desires, my destructive impulses and character flaws, my past mistakes, and the times I was victimized. It all swept over me, and I realized that there was something dark and sinister in me. I started to weep.

For the first time ever, I acknowledged how selfish I had been, and how much I had hurt important people in my life. It seemed that the pain I had inflicted on others had come back like a boomerang hitting me all at once, haunting me, and making me feel immense overwhelming guilt.

I thought about my past actions for a while, but at some point, I realized that the only thing that mattered was the present, and what I could do in the future. "I might not be able to rectify my past mistakes, but the conscious actions that I take from this point on can change things." I thought. "I have the power to create my reality, so it's my responsibility to choose between creating heaven or hell for myself and others."

I also realized that I carried around a lot of guilt, and subconsciously that guilt had turned into self-loathing. I hadn't forgiven myself for old mistakes because I felt it would be like excusing them. At that moment, I realized that the self-loathing and lack of forgiveness was forcing me to relive my mistakes over and over, and it was keeping me from moving forward and being a real force for good.

I realized that the only way to heal my old emotional wounds was to let myself off the hook, move on, and help as many people as I could. Instead of living in my dark memories, I would focus my energy forwards and outwards. It was a life-changing revelation that I was able to articulate quite well in my mind and to feel it at the bottom of my heart.

My tears subsided, and I felt a weight lift from my chest. I moved my hands around trying to lift myself off the carpet. The air felt like it was denser than usual, like my hands were cutting through a viscous fluid. I decided to stay on the carpet for a while longer.

I heard incessant dripping sounds all around me at about 4 p.m. At first, I thought the sounds were in my head, but then I realized that it was raining outside. I moved from the carpet, sat on the couch, and watched the raindrops through the window. The droplets hit the pavement and formed beautiful rainbow-colored ripples that would linger for a while then dissipate, creating room for new ripples.

In the distance, I heard dissonant musical sounds, like someone was practicing a violin but he or she was too much of an amateur to make any real music. The trees outside swayed with the wind to the tune of discordant music.

At that moment, I had an epiphany: "Life," I thought "is the perpetual process of becoming better." At the moment, I thought this was so profound, that I had to grab a notebook and write it down.

After my breakthrough and my epiphany, I was in the mood to do something productive. I went into the bathroom and started scrubbing the tub. Normally, this was the kind of chore that I agonized over and procrastinated for days, but this time, I was hyped. As I cleaned the bathroom, I was constantly distracted by the patterns formed by streaming water. It was like I could see the water in very high resolution, and my mind was focused on predicting its flow patterns.

At about half-past five, I was done cleaning the bathroom, so I decided to make a pizza from scratch. The tomatoes seemed to pulsate like they were tiny spherical animals, and this freaked me out a bit.

By 6 p.m., I started to come down. My girlfriend came home a few minutes after six, and while talking to her, I realized that most of the mescaline was gone, and there were only a few visuals left. I had a little trouble sleeping that night, but the next morning, I felt totally normal again.

FAQS

Why does mescaline get you high?

Mescaline molecules bind with specific serotonin receptors (called 5-HT 2A) in the brain, thus producing the psychoactive effects. It has a working mechanism that is similar to most other psychedelics. Scientists don't yet fully understand why activating those particular serotonin receptors results in psychedelic effects, but many have theorized that during this process, neurons (special brain cells) in the prefrontal cortex area of the brain are agitated and excited.

The prefrontal cortex is responsible for focusing your attention, controlling your impulses, coordination and controlling your behavior, and predicting how your actions will affect you and other things in your environment. So, when the prefrontal cortex is excited, these functions are affected, and you feel "high" as a result.

How long will the mescaline trip last?

Mescaline trips typically last anywhere between eight and fourteen hours. This duration varies depending on the potency of the cactus and the amount consumed. For instance, peyote typically has a higher concentration of mescaline than Peruvian torch, so a peyote trip may be on the higher end of that range, while a Peruvian torch trip may be on the lower end.

The onset time of the trip is usually between forty five and ninety minutes from the time of ingestion. This is typically followed by a one to two hour come-up period. The peak lasts anywhere between four and six hours and then there is usually a two to three hour offset period as the trip winds up.

The eight to fourteen hour trip is usually followed by a period of aftereffects (where no psychedelic effects are felt, but you still don't feel completely normal). This period typically lasts around six hours, but it may sometimes spillover into the next twenty four hours or so.

What are the side effects and symptoms of Peyote?

Peyote has both physical and mental side effects. Most effects are short term, but there are some that have the potential to be long-term.

The short-term physical side-effects of peyote include: rise in body temperature, heart palpitations, slight staggering or uncoordinated movement, general body weakness, excessive sweating, temporary increase in blood pressure, numbness in some parts of the body, feeling flushed, loss of appetite, insomnia and other sleeping difficulties, as well as severe feelings of nausea, and violent vomiting.

The short-term psychological effects may be desired or undesired, depending on the nature of the peyote trip that you want to take. These mental effects include: vivid hallucinations, feelings of euphoria, a warped sense of time, alterations in one's perceptions, feelings of panic, anxiety or paranoia, alterations in awareness, and a general inability to concentrate.

Prolonged use of Peyote may result in the following long-term effects: hallucinogen persisting perception disorder (this is a very rare condition where regular users of hallucinogens such as mescaline experience disruptive visual hallucinations even when they are completely sober), prolonged psychosis (a condition characterized by scattered thinking, periodic mood shifts, and paranoia; this is also very rare, and it's only likely to occur as a result of prolonged use of high doses of peyote).

What about tolerance and dependence of peyote?

Peyote tolerance develops very fast if it's used repeatedly in a short period of time. If you take it every day, you will start developing tolerance within three to six days. That means that you'd have to start increasing your dosage in order to get high, and you'd be stuck in a vicious cycle. It's therefore advisable to space your trips and leave a gap of at least seven to ten days between consecutive trips.

Peyote also has a cross-tolerance effect with other psychedelics such as LSD and psilocybin mushrooms. So, try to avoid taking back to back psychedelic trips even if you are using a different drug each time.

Peyote is not addictive in the conventional sense. That means it doesn't have the chemical properties required to alter the brain in order to create dependence. However, it can be "psychologically addictive." This means that even if you don't feel compelled to use it, you may still develop a dependence on it because it offers you an escape.

Psychological dependence on Peyote can negatively impact the quality of your life as well as your relationships. If it becomes a problem, you might need to seek treatment (fortunately, users won't have to deal with any nasty withdrawal symptoms).

How long does mescaline stay in your system?

Mescaline is detectable in blood for up to twenty four hours; however, if you're concerned about how long it would take before mescaline is undetectable via a drug test, then that's a different story.

Technically, the length of time within which mescaline can be detected in your system depends on the method of testing that's used to detect it. It also depends on your metabolism and other variables such as your age, your body mass, how physically active you are, how healthy you are, and how well you hydrate. So depending on those factors, it may be hard to pin down the exact time mescaline will completely exit your system.

If you are to take a urine drug test, you should know that mescaline is detectable in urine for two to three days from the point of ingestion. Mescaline is detectable in saliva for up to anywhere between one and ten days (depending on the complexity of the test that is administered). Finally, if you are subjected to a hair follicle drug test, then mescaline is detectible for up to three whole months.

AFTERWORD

Thank you for sticking with us, and for making it through to the end of *Psychoactive Cacti - The Psychedelic Effects Of Mescaline In Peyote, San Pedro, & The Peruvian Torch.* It is our sincerest hope that you have learned everything you needed to make an informed decision about mescaline.

As we part, there are a few things that we need to stress once more. First, you should remember that the decision to experiment with mescaline or any other mind-altering substance lies with you and you alone. Don't let anyone push you into doing something you don't want to.

Secondly, we need to stress the fact that mescaline is an illegal substance in most parts of the world, so if you have any intention of handling it (whether as a distributor, cultivator, or consumer), you should be aware of any (and all) legal repercussions that may result from that decision.

Finally, your safety, and the safety of those around you, should be of the utmost importance should you choose to hold or use mescaline. Keep it out of reach of children, and ensure that you don't put anyone at risk when you are tripping.

We wish you the best in whatever you do next. If you have any feedback regarding this book, we encourage you to let us know through your reviews.

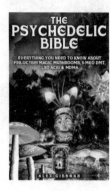

For daily posts on all things Psychedelic,
follow us on Instagram
@Psychedelic.curiosity